THE
BLACK SHEEP
THERAPIST

THE
BLACK SHEEP
THERAPIST

Integrating Spiritual & Energy-Based Modalities in Your Clinical Practice

DR. TINA VITOLO, LCSW

ILLUMIFY
MEDIA.COM

The Black Sheep Therapist

Published by
Illumify Media Global
www.IllumifyMedia.com

"Let's bring your book to life!"

Paperback ISBN: 978-1-970582-02-4

Cover design by Debbie Lewis

Printed in the United States of America

For the girl who hid to survive—
the one who swallowed her curiosity, dimmed her voice, and silenced herself for safety.
You don't have to be quiet anymore.
Thank you for being stubborn enough to question everything, bold enough to challenge others,
and brave enough to turn pain into purpose.
You are, and always will be, the heart of this work.
The world tried to silence you.
You wrote this instead.

To Dr. Kristine Baker,
whose presence made healing feel safe, real, and possible. Her impact lives on in this work—and in me.

CONTENTS

FOREWORD

This book is deeply engaging and concise, qualities which work together to mask how revolutionary it actually is. Dr. Tina Vitolo has done the work: research, thinking it through, personal introspection, and years of clinical consultation to crack the code. She now presents to us the template on how to ethically and legally integrate practices rooted in ancient esoteric systems into modern psychotherapeutic practice. The result is a template to help practitioners offer their clients a true bio-psycho-social-spiritual-energetic approach to mental well-being.

I met Tina when she responded to a Facebook comment I made, asking me if I was the same "Margaret Arnd-Caddigan" who wrote the book on clinical intuition. I knew immediately I was encountering someone with a sense of humor (no, that would be a different Margaret Arnd-Caddigan?!). As I came to know Tina and her work, I quickly became a fangirl. She's smart, intellectually thorough, completely authentic, and, of course, funny. This book is a representation of all those qualities. As you're laughing and nodding your way through the book, you may miss the incredible intellectual power it wields.

I am indeed the Margaret Arnd-Caddigan who cowrote one book and am the sole author on a second book on clinical intuition. Prior to becoming a licensed clinical social worker (LCSW), I studied the relationship between magic and religion, focusing primarily on pre- Christian European spiritual systems. I entered the practice of psychotherapy with a clear awareness that I was going to incorporate what I had learned about the power of the mind (magic) to help my clients change their minds.

Of course, this was long ago, and I had to do what I did on the down-low, especially after I completed my doctorate in social work and became an academic. I lived a double life until the end of my academic career, when I threw caution to the wind and designed research, which I completed with Marilyn Stickle, on how central intuition actually is to our profession. My academic swan song was research on psychotherapy and the paranormal. Tina has done what I could not: She has blown the doors off the closet and invited all of us "woo-woo" therapists into the light of day.

Too many people mistakenly think that those of us who embrace spirituality (especially "new age" forms of spirituality) or believe that the world is not entirely explained by material cause-and-effect answers are simple, uninformed, or unprofessional. This book is the response to every such insult. Dr. Vitolo shows the world that those of us who incorporate "alternative" healing modalities into our therapy practice must go above and beyond the level of understanding and analysis required by those who simply follow a manual. She helps the reader think and feel their way through a thorough examination of not just spit-it-back theory, but a deep dive into what therapy is and why it works. The process she leads the reader through culminates in their understanding theory as lived experience. It is through this level of understanding that the reader can then clearly articulate why and how their alternative healing strategies are an extension of the psychological theories that define our profession.

Tina has repeatedly heard what many of us have heard: "That's not ethical," or "You'll lose your license." She has masterfully pulled apart the two different issues in these statements: ethics versus law. She then lays bare the actual ethical and legal concerns with incorporating alternative and complementary practices into psychotherapy and counseling. What her massive review of the literature and work with malpractice attorneys taught her was that there is no ethical or legal prohibition against such practice. There is only the requirement that one carefully documents the steps they have taken to ensure that their practice is ethical and does not violate any state statues or licensing requirements. She has boiled this extensive work down to an accessible template so that those who follow her do not need to spend years and a small fortune to ensure they are practicing within their area of competence, their scope of practice, and in full accordance with all ethical and legal requirements.

If you are "alternative practices curious" or have been secretly (and with great trepidation) using alternative or complementary practices in your work, you must read this book. More so, you must go through the journal prompts and do the work. You will never again feel intimidated by the therapist, supervisor, or academic who disparages your work.

I promise you this: You will be so engaged by Tina's crystal-clear exposition, relate so thoroughly to her self-disclosure, and be so captivated by her no-bullshit humor that you might miss how truly revolutionary this work is. I have joked frequently that Tina is the Dr. Weil of psychotherapy/counseling. For those of you who are far younger than I, Dr. Weil is the person who almost single-handedly legitimized alternative treatments into mainstream medicine. Dr. Tina Vitolo will be remembered as the person who almost single-handedly legitimized alternative and complementary interventions into psychotherapy and counseling.

—Margaret Arnd-Caddigan, PhD, LCSW, author of *Embracing Paranormal Experiences: A Guide for Experiencers and Their Helpers*; *Holistic Psychotherapy from a Post-Materialist Perspective*; *Intuition in Therapeutic Practice: A Mind-Centered Depth Approach for Healing*; and coauthor with Marilyn Stickle of *Intuition in Psychotherapy: From Research to Practice*

INTRODUCTION

T his book is for the therapist who's done playing small.

You've been told you're "too woo-woo," "too out there," "not clinical enough." Maybe you've been side-eyed in supervision, warned to "be careful" when you brought your full self into the room. So, you toned it down. Played by the rules. Hid your knowing.

But deep down, you've always known: What you do works.

And yet, there's a fear that keeps nagging:

Will I lose my license?

What if I get reported?

Is this actually ethical?

Let's be real—most of us weren't taught how to integrate our spiritual, energetic, or intuitive gifts into therapy. In fact, we were often shamed out of them—told to follow the manual, quote the textbook, and suppress the very parts of us that clients resonate with most.

This book changes that.

The Black Sheep Therapist is your permission slip—and your protection plan. It gives you the *exact* framework I use with therapists across the country to help them bring their full, unconventional selves into their clinical work—ethically, transparently, and confidently.

Here's what you'll walk away with:

- A clear framework that aligns your spiritual or energetic tools with clinical theory,
- An informed consent framework that actually protects your license (instead of that vague EHR template),
- Research and theory to back up what you do—because we can be both intuitive and evidence-informed,
- Language that helps you describe your work with clarity and confidence,
- And most of all, the freedom to stop hiding.

If you've ever sat across from a client thinking, *I know there's more to healing than this*—you're right. If you've ever questioned whether it's *safe* to practice in the way that feels most aligned for you—this book is your map.

Each section of the book will walk you through a step-by-step process for ethical, aligned integration. You'll learn how to

Clear the Noise
Dismantle the myths you've internalized about what's unethical, out of scope, or unprofessional—and see what your license actually allows.

Define the "Unconventional"
Get clear on what we're talking about—energy healing, spiritual practices, intuitive development, and more—and how they can show up ethically in the therapy space.

Stay Grounded in Truth
Understand your legal and ethical responsibilities, how to interpret board language, and where the real risks lie.

**Anchor Your Work in Clinical Theories That
Reflect Your Values**

Learn how to identify the clinical theories that reflect your values and use them to build your Integrative Clinical Practice Framework.

Build a Real Informed Consent

Create a consent process that's robust, protective, and honest—one that speaks to who you are and what your clients can expect.

By the end, you'll have more than validation. You'll have language, clarity, confidence—and an approach that honors both your integrity *and* your soul.

How to Get the Most Out of This Book

What you'll find in these pages isn't fluff. It's not a regurgitation of tired "best practices." This is hard-earned, real-world guidance—designed to help you practice in a way that's ethical, defensible, and aligned with *your* truth.

This isn't just a book you read. It's one you work with. Highlight it. Mark it up. Use it to rewire the way you see your practice and reclaim the parts of yourself you've been told to tuck away.

As a special bonus for readers of this book, you'll receive complimentary access to my online resource—*From Magic to Method: The Black Sheep Therapist Theory Compass*—designed to help you

- Put words to the intuitive practices and approaches you're already using
- Start connecting your lived experience to solid theoretical ground

- Build confidence in talking about your work in a way that feels authentic and professional

You can access this compass by using this QR code:

Now, let me be clear: I'm not a lawyer, and this book isn't legal advice. But I *am* a licensed clinical social worker and educator who's spent years in the weeds—combing through state laws, dissecting ethical codes, cross-referencing board language, and consulting directly with attorneys and malpractice carriers. I've done the work that most therapists don't even know they *should* be doing when they start integrating unconventional practices.

You Don't Have to Do This Alone

At some point, reading may not be enough. You'll want someone to look over your documentation. To help translate your modality into clinical language. To walk beside you when you're doubting, clarifying, or building something bold.

That's why I created the Innovative Practitioner Accelerator—a high-touch coaching program designed for unconventional therapists who are done hiding and ready to practice in full alignment.

Inside IPA, you'll get

- *Personalized* support and guidance from clinicians who *get it*
- A *fully customizable*, state- and scope-compliant informed consent template
- *Weekly coaching* on clinical theory, ethical documentation, and regulatory language
- A *supportive community* of therapists walking the same integrative path
- Access to a full *digital* learning platform

Maybe you're not ready for coaching—and that's okay. Maybe you're still figuring it out. That's exactly what this book is for. It gives you the foundation, the structure, and the *why* behind the magic you already hold.

And when the time comes for deeper support, I'd love to walk with you.

You can book a free strategy call or learn more about IPA anytime at www.theblacksheepguide.com.

Because this work isn't just possible—it's powerful.

And it's time the world saw it that way.

CHAPTER 1
THE SYSTEM WASN'T BUILT FOR US—AND IT SHOWS

What They Don't Teach You in Grad School

When I first stepped into this field, I was twenty-five, fresh out of grad school, wide-eyed and allegedly ready to help people heal. Truth? I was a mess—a well-meaning, credentialed, anxious-as-hell mess. There I was in my first social work job, making a laughable income, holding therapy groups by day, drowning in my own anxiety and codependency by night. I was stuck in a toxic relationship with zero clue how to regulate my own nervous system, let alone teach someone else how to calm theirs.

I wish I could say I had an epiphany and turned it all around right then; I didn't. I stayed in different versions of that chaos for over a decade. I'll spare you the full memoir, but let's just say I got very good at playing small, hustling for scraps, and pretending that following "the rules" would somehow benefit me in the long run.

At the time, conventional therapy was the only route I knew to take to address my anxiety and relationship issues.

And honestly, some of it helped—sort of. And a lot of it didn't. It gave me just enough language and meds to function, just enough permission to keep coping—but never enough to actually feel seen or understood for who I was underneath it all.

I still remember sitting across from one of my therapists when she introduced me to the concept of thought compartmentalizing—not the most beneficial tool. She told me to picture my intrusive thoughts getting locked away in neat mental lockers, and I could control and shut down each thought as they surfaced. So I did exactly that. Locked them up and slammed the imaginary door shut. Well, I tried.

But here's the thing: Life has a way of blowing the hinges off those lockers when your pain gets too big to contain. When mine did, I realized none of that surface-level "coping" could actually hold me. It wasn't healing—it was suppression dressed up as a strategy. And that's the trap so many therapists fall into: teaching clients how to avoid their pain instead of sit with it, understand it, feel it, or transform it.

Between Two Worlds

Looking back, what I needed was a safe place to explore my heightened awareness—the part of me that always felt more. Someone to reflect back to me the things I wasn't saying, rather than regurgitating a rephrase of everything that came out of my mouth. I wasn't just "too sensitive." I was an empath—a sponge, soaking up every emotion in every room. I needed someone to see that. But nobody in a traditional office ever did.

So, I wandered. I found the spiritual community—and for the first time, people didn't flinch when I asked weird, un-Googleable questions. They didn't side-eye my intuition; they celebrated it. They didn't shame my big feelings; they held them. Finally, a space where safety and vulnerability existed at the same time??! (big sigh!)

But when I wanted to deepen that work—to understand how to bring what I was learning into my clinical work—they couldn't guide me.

So I drifted back and forth between two worlds: academic/clinical/therapeutic . . . and spiritual/mystical/intuitive. I needed both—both gave me something essential—but living in two separate lanes made me feel fragmented. *Why can't they coexist?*

The weird part? Both sides judged the shit out of the other. Some spiritual folks swore off all biomedical care—"just do holistic, meds are bad, hospitals are evil." Meanwhile, conventional practitioners called anything spiritual "pseudoscience" or "woo-woo nonsense." But hello—the evidence was literally sitting in front of them: me. My lived experience was the proof that both could be true.

Also . . . sidebar: If I'm having chest pain, do not pass me a crystal to clear my heart chakra and tell me my mind created it. Get me to the ER. Bring the crystal later. Thank you very much. Multiple truths can exist at once when it comes to health and healing. It does not have to be that deep—except, apparently, currently there is a still a rigid divide in opinions regarding the right way to heal.

The Cost of Playing It Safe

Here's what really cracked me open: As I grew more empowered in my personal healing, I felt more isolated in my professional world. The more I understood myself, the more out of place I felt in the therapy space. When I tried to talk about any of this with the so-called higher-ups, they'd glaze over or roll their eyes and pivot to the next topic. Supervisors didn't want to help me expand—they wanted me to fit the mold, check the boxes, keep my head down, and not ruffle feathers.

Honestly? It made me question whether I even wanted to be in this field anymore. The system was broken and felt impossible to change—like trying to swim straight into a wave and feeling surprised when it slams you back onto the shore. And the worst part? Even though I knew the system was messed up, I still blamed myself for struggling inside it, like the failure was mine alone. So I did what so many of us do: I learned to shut up. I split myself down the middle. My personal life stayed mine, wild and true and full of all the parts of me that actually make me good at this work. But my professional self? She stayed "safe." She stayed appropriate, clinical, small enough not to scare anyone.

And here's the thing nobody tells you about this field: Playing that split game is brutal. Try pretending for forty-plus hours a week that you don't have beliefs about healing and change. Try shutting off your soul Monday through Friday and then flipping it back on in time for the weekend. That's not just exhausting; that's how you lose the very spark you're trying to light in other people.

I knew what I was doing. I saw it. And yet . . . I still played small. I jumped from one low-paying job to the next, my only motivation being whoever was offering me the most money. Deep down, I didn't believe I'd ever feel fulfilled in this field, so all I focused on was my salary. I used it to measure my success.

I Finally Figured It Out!

Then 2018 happened—and the universe threw me a bone. After a session with my favorite intuitive and dear friend, Denise Powell, she sent me a book by Dr. Darren Weissman—*Awakening to the Secret Code of Your Mind: Your Mind's Journey* to *Inner Peace*. I remember her saying, "Your guides want you to have this book. I don't even know why I have it, but I have to send it to you."

I cracked it open, and boy did it crack something open in me. It was all about using holistic modalities and energy practices to rewire the subconscious mind. Naturally, I googled it immediately, saw there was training, and signed up on the spot. A year later I immersed myself further and started studying to become a LifeLine Technique practitioner with Dr. Darren Weissman himself.

The space and practice were beautiful: holistic, intuitive, heart-centered, spiritual, energy-based, and rooted in science. The wildest part? It reminded me of everything I learned in grad school—psychodynamic theory, Jungian ideas, attachment theory—it all started to come back and click. There was a link.

Around the same time, I was managing a neurofeedback center. Out of all my jobs working for others, this was my favorite; it was different, unique, holistic, and backed by measurable science.

One day, just for fun, I did a LifeLine Technique session on a colleague—we ran a quantitative electroencephalogram (QEEG) before and after (this is a tool that measures brain waves)—and I was blown away. What some people spent twelve weeks trying to achieve, we shifted in ninety minutes. We saw a significant increase in optimal brain-wave patterns. It blew my mind, and honestly, it lit a fire under my ass.

If this kind of accelerated healing was possible, then someone had to prove it, study it, get it out there in a way that the clinical world couldn't keep dismissing. I wanted data, evidence, language that would bridge what I knew in my gut with what the field needed to see on paper. So I applied to the

Florida Atlantic University social work doctoral program. My boss was on board—my dissertation was going to be the blueprint. Finally, I felt like I was about to put this on the map *for real* for real.

The Spiral

Then COVID hit. The clinic shut down, my carefully laid dissertation plan went out the window, and life did what life does best—shoved me right where I needed to be next. With the old plan off the table, I found myself with no safety net and no excuse not to bet on myself. So I pivoted hard and jumped into private practice.

Concurrently, while still in my doctoral program, I realized that research on holistic, complementary, and alternative interventions in mental health was still in its infancy. So my research turned to the basics: What do LCSWs know about this stuff? What's important to the field about this stuff? Meanwhile, I was building my private practice from scratch—terrified but "free." I kept my oracle cards close to my desk—only pulling them out when a client showed a glimmer of interest. Part of me thought, *When I finish this dissertation, I'll have every answer. I'll finally be the expert I need.*

Well, three years later, I walked away with a 160-page dissertation, a shiny hood, and a doctorate in social work, officially an expert in the eyes of the field. I hung up my tam, stared at my degree on the wall, and thought, *Cool. Now I can finally do what I want . . . right?*

And then that old fear slid right back in. Wait, how the hell do I actually do this? How do I bring in Human Design, LifeLine Technique, crystals, intuition, oracle cards into therapy—all the unconventional tools I know help people—without risking my license or a malpractice lawsuit?

I knew consumers wanted this—my own literature review proved it. I knew these tools were beneficial. But how to integrate them ethically and legally? *Mental crickets.*

So I panicked. I kept hoping the right clients would magically find me while I stayed under the radar. I was terrified to market myself even with my new shiny title of "Doctor." And meanwhile, I was telling my clients to show up fully, to own every piece of themselves—while, again, I was shutting down my own truth. It felt beyond ick.

I was so tired. Burned out, but still in love with the work itself. The part that drained me wasn't the clients—it was the constant second-guessing from other practitioners or even within myself. Every time I so much as hinted at weaving in the spiritual or energetic side, someone would shut it down fast:

- "That's unethical."
- "That's not evidence-based"
- "That doesn't belong in therapy."

And I just . . . took it. I didn't have the language yet to say, "Prove it." I didn't know how to point to the gaps in the code or the research. All I had back then was a gut feeling that they were wrong.

I felt like a sham. Here I was with the highest degree possible—and I still felt like an impostor. This could not be it.

So I got mad. I spiraled a bit.

I started to see the truth: The mental health system has failed us—and it's failing the people we're here to serve. I saw incredible therapists bailing for coaching because they didn't know how to do this legally and ethically. I respected it—but I also saw the giant gap it was leaving behind. If every innovative therapist jumps ship, who's left for the people who need therapy that integrates both worlds?

I kept hearing all these big conversations in the field about "transforming the foundations of mental health care" and "shifting the system." And I was like, *Hell yes, sign me up.* But whenever I asked for actual, tangible, actionable steps? Nothing. I'd get all these beautiful statements about honoring belief systems and cultural practices and moving beyond rigid, manualized empirically supported treatments (ESTs)—and again, I'm thinking, YES, *please, more of that.* That means bringing in spiritual and energy-based practices, right? Right! But then I'd ask, *How do we do that under a regulatory body? How do we do it ethically without putting our license on the line?* And again: *nothing.*

I read my professional state laws and statutes until I went cross-eyed. I literally couldn't understand what certain things meant. I emailed my board so many questions, and for fun I even started emailing boards in other states that I wasn't licensed in.

My question would go something like this:

"Research shows that there is a current increase in consumer requests for integrating complementary and alternative interventions in mental health care, and I am curious if the board has any guidelines to assist me in understanding how to ethically integrate these in my practice?"

The responses:

They would answer questions I didn't ask (by the way, to me this is the most passive aggressive thing you can do).

They would send me back a generic template with links to the same laws and statutes I'd already read.

I would not get a response at all.

And my absolute favorite: "We write the laws but can't help you interpret what they mean." I'm sorry—what in the actual fuck are you saying, like you can't be for real, can you? (they were for real).

I asked professors, colleagues—everyone just gave me a lot of encouragement, no direction, and wished me luck. Then I found a law group that specialized in helping medical professionals integrate complementary and alternative practices— jackpot! Until they charged me a grand for a forty-five-minute "chat" and told me they couldn't help. Perfect.

Spirit Came Through

I was ready to give up. But then, a classic universe move— an intuitive auditory download came through, and I heard "malpractice law group" clear as day while I was zoning out on my couch. Did I just hear that right? I grabbed my laptop, found two malpractice law firms, emailed both—and one replied immediately.

If my board couldn't help me, a malpractice lawyer definitely would. I mean who interprets the law? *Ding, ding, ding* . . . lawyers! Who better to tell me if I was moving unethically than the people specialized to go after people like me.

So we went deep: board requirements, legal language, loopholes, all of it. And you know what I found? The laws are vague on purpose. We've been brainwashed to fear the board, but once you read the fine print, you realize half of it is a riddle. But vague rules do not justify reckless behavior—it means we need a clear plan.

The union between me and this law group was honestly hilarious. Picture it: me speaking mystical, intuitive, transpersonal and them responding in pure lawyer—logical, rigid, concrete. I'll never forget one of the attorneys stumbling over how to pronounce *somatic* and needing me to explain what it actually meant.

But somehow, this unlikely duo worked. Every conversation felt like dumping out a box of puzzle pieces that didn't quite fit and then being asked to solve it daily, from scratch. Some days it made me want to scream into a pillow. So I did what I know best: focused on one piece at a time.

One day they hit me with, "You need to justify why this practice belongs in therapy."

Oh, "because it works" isn't enough? Cool, cool, love that for me.

I combed through every section they flagged. Over and over, it was the same language: clinical justification, grounded in theory, rooted in theory. Fine. Challenge accepted.

I pitched it back to them: "What if I map out my entire integrative theoretical framework—lay out exactly what I believe about healing, explain how each modality fits within it, show real benefits, real risks, cite the research, back it up with my training receipts—all of it? Would that check every box?"

They wanted to see it in black and white. So I sat my ass down and drafted a ten-page addendum to my informed consent—every detail, every angle, nothing hidden.

When I sent it, I asked them point blank, "Am I gucci?"

I'll never forget the relief when they came back with, "I have no idea what else you could possibly add."

I could've cried—partly because I finally had a clear answer, partly because I was done paying them. Ten grand just to help me read and interpret—sheesh. But in the end? Worth it.

The Innovative Practitioner Accelerator Was Born

What I walked away with wasn't just a fancy document. It was a tangible, actionable, proven framework that showcased my knowledge, my due diligence, and my clinical integrity. It checked every interpretive law box. It let me merge my modalities into my therapy practice—without losing my alignment, my beliefs, or my license. It turned my informed consent into an actual *informed* consent. That's real professional freedom. And I fucking loved that feeling.

I knew I couldn't keep this to myself, so I leaned on my dear friend and innovator Carly Hill, the brilliance behind *The Coach Intensive*, for guidance. She has always been my "yes" girl, and she was all in for this one. I wanted to share everything I'd learned—to empower other unconventional, innovative, trailblazing black sheep therapists. To give them a voice, a seat at the table, and tangible tools to do what we all know is possible: to bring their whole damn selves into the room without sacrificing professionalism and saying, "I don't care; if they take my license, they take my license." No.

Because here's the thing: For too long this field has made us feel like we have to choose. Be "clinical" *or* be intuitive. Follow the manual *or* trust our knowing. Be ethical *or* be who we really are. And that's the lie I refuse to pass down to another generation of therapists.

This work is not either/or. It's both/and. It's science and soul. Research and ritual. Data and depth. Structure and spirit. We can hold all of it clearly, transparently, and ethically, and finally do what we came here to do: help people heal in a way that actually works.

That's the entire heartbeat behind the book you are holding in your hands. It's what helped me develop my Innovative Practitioner Accelerator Program. Not theory for theory's sake. Not fluff. Real, actionable, regulatory, sound tools to back your magic up with clinical muscle—so you can practice out loud, protect your license, and never again feel like you have to shut down part of yourself just to keep a seat in this field.

At the time I'm writing this book, I've helped so many unconventional therapists step into their voice, realign with their purpose, craft their vision, and claim real professional freedom in their therapy practice. Some of them have gone on to write, train, teach, speak on big stages, and let me tell you, an empowered unconventional therapist is a force. Watch out, world.

It's honestly the most beautiful thing to witness: these brilliant humans shifting from small, confused, frustrated, and hidden practitioners to clear and confident badasses. One of my favorite parts is showing them that nothing about their magic or process needs to be stripped away.

We just need language. We just need to anchor it in theory.

The real gold? We deep-dive into their story—their lived experience, their wounds, their uniqueness, their wisdom—and use it as the key to see who they really are as a practitioner. Understanding and owning that identity is everything. It makes them feel seen, heard, and celebrated . . . something this field loves to talk about but *rarely* delivers on.

Do I help you cover your ass as well? Well, yeah. But that's not the heart of it. I'm about the alignment. The self-understanding. The real-life application. Then we wrap it all up in your informed consent so you're protected on paper too.

I want you to have tools—not just big ideas. Real steps. Clear guidelines. I want you to know the truths and the myths. I want you to move with integrity. I want you to stand unshakable in your practice style when people challenge you. Because they will. And when they do, you won't shrink. You'll know exactly why you practice the way you do.

You will not flinch—you'll educate. Every question will become an opportunity for you to stand taller, share your truth, protect your work, and show the world exactly what's possible when a Black Sheep Therapist refuses to stay hidden.

You fired up? Me too! LFG!

CHAPTER 2
MYTH-BUSTING MENTAL HEALTH—
WHAT THEY NEVER TELL YOU

Let's start by clearing something up: When I use terms like unconventional, nontraditional, energy-based, or spiritual practices, I'm not actually saying these are "new" or "fringe." I'm saying they've only been made to look that way inside rigid Western mental health frameworks.

In fact, many of the modalities and interventions I'm referring to, like energy healing, ancestral ritual, mediumship, somatic movement, and intuitive development, have been around for centuries. They are rooted in culture, lineage, and lived experience. They've shaped the way entire communities understand illness, healing, spirit, and the human condition. What's unconventional is the field of psychotherapy treating these traditions like they don't belong.

But here's the challenge: When you're practicing under a regulatory body, which we are, you need language. You need definition. You need research.

And these practices—rich, complex, often subjective and experiential—rarely come with an abundance of easily accessible peer-reviewed research articles or nicely packaged manualized steps. That doesn't make them less valid. It makes them harder to mainstream.

In my own dissertation, I explored how social workers perceive these practices and how hard it is even to name them without feeling like you're either appropriating culture or erasing nuance. The best language I could find that aligned with a social work and mental health perspective was complementary and alternative interventions (Vitolo, Cooley, and Weissman 2023).

Complementary and alternative medicine (CAM) is defined as a diverse group of health and medical care systems, practices, and products not considered part of conventional (allopathic) medicine (National Center for Complementary and Integrative Health [NCCIH], n.d.). But in therapy, we don't use the word *medicine*. We're not prescribing. So in my research, I shifted the language from "medicine" to "intervention" to reflect the supportive, integrative nature of what we're actually doing in clinical practice.

According to current research, complementary and alternative medicine (CAM) falls under five umbrella categories (Armson et al. 2019; Clarke et al. 2015; Institute of Medicine 2005; National Center for Complementary and Integrative Health n.d.):

1. Alternative medical systems: naturopathy, traditional Chinese medicine
2. Biology-based interventions: supplements, herbs, dietary changes
3. Mind–body interventions: hypnosis, meditation, breathwork, biofeedback
4. Body-based interventions: yoga, acupuncture, massage, chiropractic
5. Energy interventions: Reiki, therapeutic touch, qigong

Still, even those categories don't tell the whole story. Where does mediumship fit? What about intuitive sensing? Ancestral altar work? Astrology? These practices don't always fall neatly into one of the five CAM umbrellas. And some of them, like what I witnessed in my own family, aren't easy to name at all.

Both of my grandfathers were healers in Italy. But even now, no one in my family can fully explain what that meant. There was no certificate on the wall, no formal training to point to—just a deep knowing, a reverence, a practice that lived in the body and in the land. I still don't have the language to capture it, but I know it was real. I know it mattered. And I know I carry it with me.

The problem is, when you're a therapist operating under a regulatory board, "I know it in my bones" isn't enough. We need language. We need frameworks. Not to erase the soul of these practices but to honor them, protect them, and make room for them inside a system that was never built to hold them. I often joke that I'm trying to translate fifth-dimensional language into a third-dimensional world—because so much of what we work with energetically or spiritually doesn't fit neatly into the linear, rigid frameworks our field often demands.

We have to acknowledge that language itself is a limitation and still, we need it. We need structure, documentation, and transparency, not to strip these practices of their soul but to ethically translate them across the legal and professional systems we have chosen to work within.

Even with limited research, what we do know is this: CAM use is one of the fastest-growing consumer trends in the United States (McEwen 2015). And the number one reason people turn to CAM? Alignment. These interventions resonate deeply with their personal values, spiritual beliefs, and worldview, much more so than interventions grounded solely in the biomedical model (El-Olemy et al. 2014; Islahudin, Shahdan, and Mohamad-Samuri 2017; McFadden, Hernández, and Ito 2010).

So, when therapists dismiss these practices as pseudoscience or "woo," they're not just dismissing interventions; they're dismissing the very belief systems that guide their clients' healing journeys.

And that, my friend, is the real ethical issue.

Myth #1: "It's unethical."

It's always struck me as strange: We're told over and over that therapists must demonstrate cultural humility, honor the diverse belief systems of our clients, and hold space for different worldviews. But then, in the same breath, we're told that integrating spiritual or energy-based practices into therapy is unethical.

Wait . . . what?

You can't preach inclusivity and cultural humility, then penalize therapists for integrating practices rooted in their clients' lived experiences, especially when you've given them no ethical road map to do it right.

I used to be so triggered when I would hear people say this, but here's what changed: I started actually reading the laws, the ethics codes, the professional conduct rules—not the blog posts or gossip threads, definitely not the Facebook comments—the real documents.

And guess what?

There is nothing in any professional mental health code of ethics that says the use of complementary or alternative interventions in clinical practice is inherently unethical. Nothing. In fact, language surrounding the treatments and modalities in general is minimal and extremely vague.

What is unethical?

- Misrepresenting your qualifications
- Making unsupported claims
- Failing to explain risks/benefits
- Practicing outside your competency
- Having sexual relationships with your clients
- Violating communication standards of personal health information

You know, things you should be avoiding anyway.

But to move forward I have to distinguish between ethics violations (what your professional code prohibits) and licensure violations (what your state board or regulatory authority enforces).

Just because something isn't illegal doesn't mean it's ethical and vice versa. And then there's a third layer: scope of practice. Most boards don't even define exactly what is or isn't in scope—they leave it vague. Which leaves many therapists confused, scared, silent, and stuck (exactly where I was and where I presume you may be).

Let's take a closer look at four of the most widely recognized professional organizations in the field of mental health: the American Counseling Association (ACA), the National Association of Social Workers (NASW), the American Association for Marriage and Family Therapy (AAMFT), and the American Psychological Association (APA).

I don't like to rely on hearsay or assumptions about what's "ethical"; 1 want the source. What do they *really* say about integrating nontraditional or emerging practices? Well, let's break it down.

The ACA *Code of Ethics* states that "when providing services, counselors use techniques/procedures/modalities that are grounded in theory and/or have an empirical or scientific foundation" (American Counseling Association 2014, C.7.a). It goes on to clarify that "when counselors use developing or innovative techniques/procedures/modalities, they explain the potential risks, benefits, and ethical considerations of using such techniques" and that they "work to minimize any potential risks or harm" (American Counseling Association 2014, C.7.b).

The NASW *Code of Ethics* acknowledges the reality of emerging practices and offers clear guidance: "When generally recognized standards do not exist with respect to an emerging area of practice, social workers should exercise careful judgment and take responsible steps (including appropriate education, research, training, consultation, and supervision) to ensure the competence of their work and to protect clients from harm" (National Association of Social Workers 2021, 4.01(c)).

The AAMFT *Code of Ethics* emphasizes that "marriage and family therapists ensure that their work is based on established knowledge, including empirically supported treatments relevant to their discipline and the clients they serve," and that they "make available to clients accurate professional information about their qualifications, including educational background, experience, theoretical orientation, and professional affiliations" (American Association for Marriage and Family Therapy 2015, 2.5, 3.9).

The APA *Code of Ethics* acknowledges that psychologists may sometimes serve clients in areas outside their immediate expertise, stating, "When psychologists are asked to provide services to individuals for whom appropriate mental health services do not exist, psychologists with closely related prior training or experience may provide such services in order to ensure that services are not denied if they make a reasonable effort to obtain the competence required by using relevant research, training, consultation, or study" (American Psychological Association 2017, 2.01(f)).

Notice what's *not* in there? A list of banned modalities. No code of ethics says, "Don't integrate Reiki," or "Tarot in psychotherapy is unethical." What they say is this: Know what you're doing, be trained, be transparent, understand the risks, use your judgment, ground it in clinical theory, and be transparent when obtaining informed consent.

The real issue is that most therapists have never been taught *how* to prove that they are doing this. How do you write an informed consent for something like breathwork or justify the use of intuition in your practice? Don't worry, that's what this book is here to fix.

Navigating the Legal Landscape: What Your State Actually Says

Now, I know what you're thinking: *Okay, cool, the ethics codes sound pretty open-ended. But what about the* law? Here's the truth: I can't include the full legal statutes for all fifty states in this book. If I tried, this book would never be finished.

I am currently conducting research on this very issue—examining how the language of scope of practice, application of methods, and lists of prohibited or excluded practices are written across the licensing boards for psychologists, social workers, marriage and family therapists, and professional/mental health counselors throughout the United States.

Why? Because I'm tired of hearing that the integrative, adjunctive use of spiritual, energy-based, evidence-informed, or emerging practices has "no place" in mental health. That narrative has gone unchallenged for too long. I intend to prove otherwise in black and white, straight from the statutes themselves.

For now, I'll show you how to start your own exploration: where to find this language, how to interpret it, and what examples reveal about just how much room exists for innovation and integration within our profession. Let's get into some state examples.

Alabama's legal definition of clinical social work emphasizes "the professional application of social work theory and methods to the treatment and prevention of psychosocial dysfunction . . . based on knowledge of one or more theories of human development within a psychosocial context" (Alabama Legislature 2024, §34-30).

Notice what's *not* in there? No requirement for "manualized treatments," "evidence-based modalities," or "scientific proof." What it *does* highlight is theory and competence—which means that if you can articulate your work through a theoretical lens, you are not stepping out of bounds.

Florida defines mental health counseling as "the use of scientific and applied behavioral science theories, methods, and techniques for the purpose of describing, preventing, and treating undesired behavior and enhancing mental health and human development," noting that it is "based on the person-in-situation perspectives derived from research and theory" (Florida Legislature 2024, §491).

This definition highlights a wide range of domains grounded in research and theory, but it leaves substantial room for interpretation in how those concepts are applied in practice.

You'll also notice that there's no hard line drawn around "evidence-based only." There's nothing that excludes spiritual or energy-based modalities—as long as you can justify your work using theoretical foundations.

Minnesota law defines mental health services as those designed to "alleviate symptoms, change or reduce disturbed patterns of behavior, enhance intrapsychic awareness, and increase the ability of the individual to adapt to and cope with internal and external stress," noting that these services "must use interpersonal, intrapsychic, or behavioral methods" (Minnesota Legislature 2024, §148B).

This definition is a powerful reminder that state law often prioritizes function and clinical intention over rigid methods. Nowhere does it demand therapists use only "evidence-based" or mainstream interventions. Instead, it leaves room for a wide range of modalities—including those often considered unconventional—as long as they are delivered competently, ethically, and in service of therapeutic goals.

What matters most is the purpose: to reduce distress, increase awareness, and support adaptation. And the method of delivery must align with one or more recognized therapeutic orientations—interpersonal, intrapsychic, or behavioral. For therapists working at the intersection of clinical and holistic care, definitions like this don't restrict.

They affirm.

What I hope you are getting from this is my original point: Most boards are not creating rigid lists of what is or isn't allowed regarding mental health practice. Instead, they're asking you to operate from a foundation of recognized theory, demonstrated competency, and clear therapeutic intent. The law isn't requiring your work to be conventional; it's requiring it to be clinically grounded, ethically delivered, and justifiable if questioned. And honestly, it should be.

If you can clearly articulate why you're using a particular approach, how you're trained in it, and what clinical purpose it serves—and you're staying within the bounds of your education, training, and supervision—then you're likely already practicing in alignment with what most boards expect.

If you are doubting me, please check for yourself. Every mental health license type includes a statutory definition of practice. That means you can—and absolutely *should*—look up how your state defines terms like *counseling, clinical social work, marriage and family therapy, psychotherapy,* and *mental health treatment.*

> *Pro tip:* Open your state's practice act or code of ethics as a PDF, hit Control + F (or Command + F on a Mac), and try search terms such as ethics, definitions, research, empirical, evidence-based, scientific, alternative, scope, competence, informed consent, excluded, prohibit, unethical, and empirically supported.

Go ahead. I'll wait. You might be surprised by what you find and more importantly what you *don't* find.

As someone currently knee-deep in a fifty-state research dive, I have to laugh sometimes—not because it's funny but because it's so revealing.

In many states, the section on what constitutes clinical practice is barely three sentences long, while the section on sexual misconduct reads like a legal novella. In others, you'll find a whole paragraph dedicated to re-explaining who can call themselves a "licensed social worker"—as if the title itself might spontaneously combust without sufficient regulation.

Sadly, it's not a joke. It's a pattern. These laws weren't written to guide innovation; they were written to react to misconduct. And that tells us a lot about what's *missing* from the regulatory conversation—and why it's so critical for us to read between the lines.

So, to wrap it up, we've been conditioned to think these words are carved in stone across all our laws, but most aren't.

And when they are there, the definitions are often vague or wide open to interpretation. This is why people shout, "That's unethical!" without ever being able to point you to the damn law. The law lives in these documents, not in opinions, not in Facebook comments, not in licensing exam prep books. If you're going to practice differently, you've got to read it for yourself. Period.

Myth #2: "It's not evidence based."

God, I hate this one—mostly because people throw it around without knowing what they're saying. "Evidence-based" and "empirically supported treatments" are not the same thing. Allow me to explain.

Empirically supported treatments (ESTs) are manualized protocols that have been rigorously tested through randomized controlled trials (RCTs). Think CBT, DBT, EMDR. They've got comparison groups, symptom reduction stats, the whole nine. Cool.

But despite how hard ESTs are pushed in the therapy world, they are *not* required by any state law or code of ethics—which makes you wonder why they're treated like gospel? In my opinion, that's the lingering shadow of the Flexner Report, which in the early 1900s slammed non-biomedical models as "quackery" and embedded the biomedical mindset deep into our profession (Flexnor 1910).

What followed? Capitalistic, insurance-driven, rigid systems that still dominate mental health today. And we have been stuck in this mentality ever since.

But let's talk about evidence-based practice (EBP)—which I do ride for. EBP is a broader framework built on three pillars:

- The best available research
- Clinical expertise and competency

- Client preferences, values, and lived experience (We'll come back to this third one later when we talk about theory.)

This definition comes directly from the APA's Presidential Task Force on Evidence-Based Practice (American Psychological Association Presidential Task Force on Evidence-Based Practice 2006). However, I believe there are misconceptions within each of these pillars, so I would like to break them down one by one.

Research isn't limited to randomized controlled trials (RCTs). In fact, our understanding of what "counts" as valid research is far broader and more inclusive than many clinicians are taught. When someone claims something "isn't evidence-based," they're often thinking narrowly, ignoring the entire spectrum of research that contributes to our field. What counts as "evidence":

- *Meta-analyses and systematic reviews* synthesize findings from dozens (sometimes hundreds) of studies. These offer powerful insights by showing patterns across large bodies of research, not just a single study's outcome.
- *Quasi-experimental studies* are common in real-world research when randomization isn't possible. They still use comparison groups and control for variables, offering valuable evidence—especially when working in complex or community-based settings.
- *Case series and single-subject designs* are often used when the population is small or the intervention is new or specialized. These studies are especially relevant when working with rare conditions or

individualized interventions, and they offer a detailed view of client progress over time.

- *Qualitative studies* include interviews, focus groups, ethnographies, and narrative analysis and are especially important in trauma-informed, community-based, or culturally rooted practices. These studies highlight meaning, depth, and lived experience, which is often what CAIs seek to honor.

- *Peer-reviewed theoretical papers* are sometimes dismissed, but when they cite research-based mechanisms (like nervous system regulation, trauma processing, or consciousness studies), they help bridge clinical application with scientific inquiry.

- *Practice-based evidence* is the documentation of real outcomes in clinical practice. If you're tracking results over time in your own caseload—symptom reduction, client-reported progress, functional changes—that's data. And increasingly, it's being recognized as a form of evidence in its own right.

The truth is, evidence isn't one-size-fits-all. Especially for practices that emerge from cultural, spiritual, or relational contexts, the research will look different, but that doesn't make it any less valid. We need a wider lens, not a narrower rulebook.

So, when I tell you I've seen *peer-reviewed* research on tarot/oracle cards, crystal healing, chakra balancing, Reiki, pendulums, mediumship, and intuition—you might be surprised. Let me share a few shots across the bow:

- Reiki: A 2021 *systematic review* published in *Holistic Nursing Practice* found that Reiki significantly reduced symptoms of stress, anxiety, and depression in mental health settings (Morero et al. 2021).

- Chakra Meditation: A 2020 study in the *International Journal of Social Welfare Promotion and Management* found that participants experienced marked reductions in anxiety and increased emotional well-being after chakra-focused meditation practices (Lim and Lee 2020).
- Intuition in Therapy: *Intuition in Psychotherapy* by Stickle and Arnd-Caddigan (2019) is a qualitative study of practicing clinicians. Their findings? Intuition can powerfully inform diagnostic insight, therapeutic resonance, and case formulation—all while remaining ethically grounded in the clinical process (Stickle and Arnd-Caddigan 2019).

Here's my metaphor: Research is like the Olympics—the gold medal (RCTs) gets the spotlight, but every other level of participation adds value. Case studies, qualitative findings are straight-up wins on the path to integration. And with many therapists struggling under burnout, low pay, and endless paperwork, expecting gold-medal research from every modality is unrealistic. But contributions in any form matter.

My stance: I'm for scientific backing, and I don't drink the Kool-Aid that believes only manualized, RCT-research therapies count. EBP means honoring where the evidence is and building integrity, training, and transparency around it.

So next time someone scoffs, "That's not evidence-based," ask them what *exactly* they mean and whether they can point to that expectation in the laws or ethics codes. *Cough Cough* They won't find it.

Myth #3: "Spiritual and energy-based practices have NO place in therapy."

Says who?

Not your clients.

A 2023 study of over five hundred mental health consumers found that 72 percent reported using some form of complementary or alternative care, and more than half said that combining CAM with medication was more effective than using medication alone (Clossey et al. 2023). That's not a niched group. That's the majority.

And they're not alone.

National CDC data show that over 36 percent of U.S. adults use complementary health approaches, with especially high usage among women and among specific racial and ethnic groups depending on the modality (Clarke et al. 2015). These trends don't just signal dissatisfaction with conventional care—they point to a growing desire for approaches that align with people's healing philosophies, cultural context, and personal definitions of wellness.

Across multiple studies, one truth keeps showing up: Consumers, especially older adults, women, and communities of color, are actively choosing spiritual practices, herbal medicine, and mind-body therapies to address anxiety, depression, and chronic stress (Astin 1998; Bishop and Lewith 2010; Cherniack, Senzel, and Pan 2008; Johnson et al. 2018). These aren't impulsive or uninformed choices. They're intentional, born from experience, and guided by values (hmm . . . sounds like one of the pillars of evidence-based practice).

Clients aren't chasing trends. They're seeking real relief in ways that resonate with their identities and lived realities.

So why does the mental health field still treat integrative care like it's taboo?

The research tells us something else too: When practitioners personally resonate with or use these approaches themselves, they're far more likely to welcome conversations about them in the therapy room, make referrals, and affirm the tools their clients already value (Armson et al. 2019; Aveni et al. 2017; DeSylvia et al. 2011). But when they don't? Silence. Dismissal. Distance. Clients pick up on that quickly—and many stay quiet to avoid being shamed or misunderstood.

And that silence? It doesn't protect ethics. It fractures trust.

How the hell is that person-centered care? (*Insert my big sigh.*)

Therapists are shamed all the time for using or even being curious about integrative approaches. If they're being dragged on public social media threads for naming their work with energy, spirit, or intuition—what do you think is happening behind closed doors with the clients these "ethical" textbook therapists serve? I mean, I can't know for sure, but I can sure guess.

We say we value cultural humility and inclusivity. But let's be honest: Too many in this field weaponize clinical language to police what "real therapy" should look like. And if that therapy doesn't mirror a whitewashed, manualized, diagnosis-driven model, it's dismissed as dangerous, unethical, or unprofessional.

That's not protection. That's projection.

Clients are already bringing their full selves into the room. When therapists shut down, avoid, or dismiss the parts of clients rooted in spiritual belief or ancestral practice, we're not just missing an opportunity; we're breaking rapport. We're telling them that the parts that bring them strength, hope, and meaning don't belong here.

And that has never been what this field and practice has been about. And yet here we are.

CHAPTER 3
THE FRAMEWORK—AKA HOW TO STOP PLAYING BY THEIR RULES

After sitting down with lawyers and combing through state laws, administrative codes, and board regulations, one thing became painfully clear. It's not enough to say, "Don't worry, I'm following the rules." You have to *prove it*.

And sure—on the surface, that might sound simple.

But here's the truth: The "rules" are vague, disjointed, and open to interpretation.

You think you understand one section . . .

Then a few lines later, you're reading something that contradicts it completely.

So you reach out for help—and what do you get?

Not guidance.

Not clarity.

Just a polite email saying, "We cannot interpret the statute for you."

So now you're left wondering, *What does proof even look like in a system that won't define its terms?*

How do you demonstrate ethical care when the language is built on gray areas?

How do you move with confidence when the people in charge won't tell you where the boundaries are?

These questions hit me like a brick.

I had always led with integrity. My intentions were solid.

But in the eyes of the system? That didn't mean a thing if I couldn't *prove it*.

So I did what most people in this field don't have time—or support—to do: I built it.

A document that made my alignment visible. It showed the following:

I read and understood my state's laws, regulations, and scope definitions.

I reviewed my professional code of ethics *line by line*.

I made informed, well-reasoned interpretations of both.

And I built *real systems* in my practice that reflected those interpretations—transparently, intentionally, and defensibly.

Was it overwhelming? Absolutely.

But that was the turning point.

It's when I stopped hoping I was doing things right . . . and started *knowing* I could defend every inch of my work.

That's the moment my ethical and regulatory-aligned framework was born.

And now? My hope is that it does the same for you.

The Basic Informed Consent

Now, before we get to that framework, let's pause and talk about what I call the "illusion of the basic informed consent." You know the one—it's the template you bought for ninety-nine dollars, or the generic form your EHR software gave you and told you to upload. Most therapists assume this covers their bases. But in reality these documents often fall short of what your specific license, state, and ethical body require.

Let's run a quick checklist of what should be in an informed consent *at minimum*:

- Overview of services
- Education, certification, and licensure
- General risks and benefits of therapy
- Delivery of services (telehealth, in-person benefits/ risks, etc.)
- Recording and documentation policies
- Grounds for declining or terminating treatment
- Scheduling and cancellation policies
- Fee schedule and payment policies
- Good Faith Estimates (GFE) and No Surprises Act
- Insurance status (in-network vs. out-of-network)
- Confidentiality and limits to confidentiality
- Protection of Personal Health Information (PHI)
- Communication policy (phone, email, text, client portal)
- Social media and dual relationship policy
- Privacy policy and records access/keeping

If you're reading this like, "Shoot, I don't even know if all of this is in mine," go check it. And that's not even the full list.

Because here's the thing: Some states have highly specific requirements. Some require that you provide a live link where clients can verify your licensure status, other states require that you provide clients with contact information for where they can report ethical concerns, and others don't mention the need to state contact information at all. Some states want your degrees, credentials, affiliations, license numbers—all printed out in black and white. Others? Nada.

So, if you've ever felt like it's impossible to find a one-size-fits-all informed consent, you're absolutely right. And that's exactly why I stopped relying on templates.

Instead, I started building my own, customized to each therapist I work with by actually combing through their specific state statutes, rules, laws, admin codes, and professional ethics codes line by line.

Because here's the hard truth no one tells you: Being in private practice isn't just about helping people heal—it's also about knowing how to run an ethical and legally compliant business. And no, grad school didn't teach you this. Most of us learn through Facebook threads, random horror stories, or frantically googling the term "Good Faith Estimate" at two a.m. It's exhausting. It's overwhelming. And it doesn't have to be that way.

If you've made it this far, I want to acknowledge that you're not just reading a book. You're starting to shift the way you see your responsibility as a regulated professional. And that's a big deal.

Now, let me walk you through the exact framework I developed to help unconventional black sheep therapists like you and me turn vague legal language into clear, actionable protections—for both your clients *and* your license.

This is the foundation I use with every clinician I work with. Think of it as your ethical bridge: a way to honor your magic *and* meet your professional obligations. I'll outline the framework here, and then we'll go deeper into each step in the chapters that follow.

The Ethical Integration Framework

1. Remain Within Your Scope of Practice

Before you bring any complementary, alternative, spiritual, or energy-based modality into your therapy practice, the first question you need to ask is, *Does this fall within the legal boundaries of my license?*

Scope of practice isn't about how passionate you are, how transformative a modality has been in your own life, or even how effective it's been with clients. It's a legal threshold—set by your state and your professional license—that defines what you're permitted to do as a mental health provider. Just because something feels aligned clinically doesn't automatically mean it's authorized legally.

Remember, most state boards and national ethical codes don't spell things out with a tidy list of dos and don'ts. Instead, they lean on vague terms like "principles and values of the profession," "theoretically grounded," or "consistent with professional standards." That's where things get blurry—and where your ethical interpretation, clear documentation, and clinical rationale become essential.

To stay within your scope while incorporating complementary and alternative interventions (CAIs), the key is integration. What I call the "both/and approach"—using these practices not as stand-alone services but as adjunctive practices—to complement, enhance, and deepen your clinical work. When done thoughtfully, this approach strengthens—not stretches—the ethical integrity of your practice.

In chapter 4, we are going to unpack the real meaning of *scope of practice*—and how it differs from *competency*, even though the two are often confused. We have already walked through some examples pulled from state and ethical boards, but we will dive even deeper into how integration is the ethical path forward—not as a workaround but as a clinically grounded strategy.

2. Prove Your Competency

Before you bring any complementary, alternative, spiritual, or energy-based practice into the therapy space, make sure you've been trained in it. Read that again. Please.

Personal experience matters, but professional competency is nonnegotiable. Certifications, supervised practice, continuing education—your training and expertise should match the depth of what you're offering.

In chapter 4, I'll walk you through what counts as *proof* of competency when you're integrating a complementary, spiritual, or energy-based modality into clinical work. This isn't just about having experience—it's about being able to justify it clearly, ethically, and in alignment with your license.

3. Build Your Integrative Clinical Practice Framework (ICPF)

In chapter 5, I will walk you through a comprehensive process on how to identify the clinical theories and frameworks that actually reflect your values, story, and practice style. I will then show you how to use those theories to craft client-facing language that clearly communicates what you do, how you help, and what your clients can expect from you.

I will break down why clinical theory is the *missing link* when it comes to ethically and effectively integrating complementary, spiritual, and energy-based practices into your clinical work. You'll learn the difference between theories and modalities—how one provides the foundation while the other is the expression—and why conflating the two creates confusion. I'll guide you through my reverse-engineered process for uncovering the theories that already live in your story, your clinical intuition, and the way you naturally show up in the therapy room.

This is where your personal journey, professional training, and lived experience come together to form your Integrative Clinical Practice Framework (ICPF)—a living, breathing map of your unique approach to healing. This process is deep, clarifying, and honestly, a little uncomfortable yet sacred. It's about finally giving language and legitimacy to the work you've been doing all along.

4. Speak Transparently About Your Modality and Approach

Don't just say you "use Reiki" or "work somatically." Describe what that looks like *in your practice*. Break it down in everyday language, and get specific about applications and potential benefits. What are you actually doing? What's your process? Are touch, sound, scents involved? This isn't just for your informed consent—it helps your clients trust the process and helps your regulatory body clearly see your process.

This is about creating a full, transparent appendix that outlines what you do, how you do it, and why. In chapter 9, we'll break down how to describe your interventions in plain, everyday language—covering what the process looks like, how it's applied, what the client can expect, and what (if any) tools or senses are involved, such as touch, sound, or scent. You'll also learn how to include cultural and lineage-informed acknowledgments, while highlighting the benefits you witness and aim for in session. This step builds clarity, integrity, and trust—for your clients and for the board.

5. Acknowledge Risks and Limitations

Every intervention—clinical or complementary—has potential risks. Don't avoid them. Speak to them clearly. This builds trust and transparency, and it protects your client's right to informed choice.

In chapter 9, we'll explore how to name the potential risks, limitations, and contraindications of the complementary and alternative practices you use—without fear or defensiveness. You'll learn how to do this in a way that empowers client choice, builds clinical trust, and strengthens ethical integrity. We'll break down how to document risk in plain language, what kinds of disclosures matter most (especially for spiritual or energy-based interventions), and how to strike a balance between informed consent and honoring the nuance of your work. I'll also give you examples of how to reflect on your own blind spots, clarify boundaries, and communicate scope without undermining the power of the modality.

6. Align Your Modalities Through a Theoretical Lens

This is gold. Once you've identified your core theories and modalities, it's time to build the bridge between them. Get clear on your "both/and approach": What do you bring from the clinical world? What do you bring from the spiritual or unconventional realm? And how do you *talk about* that fusion?

If you can't describe it clearly, your clients and your board won't understand it either. This is how you move your work from "woo" to within your scope: by grounding it in theory.

That's what the Clinical Fusion Blueprint is all about. In chapter 10, you'll learn how to map your holistic practices—like Reiki, tarot, or aromatherapy—onto established clinical theories using clear, evidence-informed language. We'll walk through real examples so you can confidently explain how your tools align with your purpose, outcomes, and ethical scope.

7. Back It Up with Research

Whether it's peer-reviewed studies, emerging evidence, or qualitative findings—gather support for the practices you use. You don't need a dissertation, but you do need to show that your work is grounded in more than intuition alone. Additionally, this also proves your due diligence in being aware of the latest research available on the modalities that you are integrating.

You might be surprised by how much research already exists to support the practices you use. In chapter 10, I'll walk you through how to find relevant studies, distinguish peer-reviewed articles from popular media, and assess the strength and limitations of the evidence. We'll also talk about how to cite this research meaningfully in your documentation—not to overmedicalize your work but to demonstrate professional due diligence, cultural awareness, and clinical responsibility. This step helps you stay informed, confident, and rooted in evidence as the field continues to evolve.

So, if you're sitting here thinking, *Damn, this is a lot,* you're right. It is. But this is what it looks like to stop begging the system for clarity and start creating your own. You've played by their rules long enough and where has that gotten you? Confused. Cautious. Second-guessing work that's actually changing lives. That ends here. The framework you're about to step into isn't about compliance for compliance's sake. It's about taking back your power—learning the rules well enough to bend them with precision, protect your license with receipts, and practice with the freedom they told you wasn't possible. Welcome to the part where we stop shrinking and start building our own damn blueprint.

CHAPTER 4
INTEGRATION IN ACTION—TURNING REBEL IDEAS INTO REAL PRACTICE

People often misunderstand me when I talk about integrating spiritual or energy-based practices into therapy.

When they hear that a clinician wants to integrate Reiki into their practice, they may immediately picture a full sixty-minute, hands-on session—table, crystals, music, the whole nine yards. Or when they hear "oracle cards" or "tarot cards," they may assume it's a totally separate, nonclinical service being offered on the side. They imagine an individual switching hats between "therapist" and "healer," toggling roles depending on the day.

Let me be clear: That's not what I'm describing. At all.

There is no separation.

No replacement of clinical knowledge and applications. No toggling back and forth between licensed therapist and spiritual practitioner. That would be a dual relationship, and it's not what we're doing here. Later in this book, I will discuss how this will look in your actual informed consent, but for now let me just break down this concept.

What I'm talking about is integration—true integration—where your clinical knowledge stays front and center, and complementary tools are brought in as part of the therapy process to support, deepen, or accelerate healing: It's both/and, not either/or.

These practices aren't competing with your therapeutic work. They're enhancing it. And when done ethically, they're aligned with the same purpose: client transformation.

Now, this can look different for different practitioners, and that's not only okay; it's welcomed. I believe the most ethical work is often the most personalized. When your clinical decisions are guided by a deep understanding of your client's needs *and* your own attunement, training, and values, you create a practice that is rooted in integrity.

Ethical work doesn't mean following a script. It means being thoughtful, intentional, and clear about *how* and *why* you show up the way you do and making sure that your tools, whether spiritual, energetic, and/or empirically supported, are used with clarity, competence, and care.

Scope of Practice

Another common area of confusion is the difference between scope of practice and competency. While they are not the same, both must be clearly understood—and actively upheld in clinical practice.

To define it a little further, your scope of practice is *what you are legally and ethically allowed to do* based on your professional title. This is defined by your license type (LCSW, LMFT, LPC, LMHC), your state laws, and professional code of ethics.

You know your girl loves examples.

As an LCSW, you are *allowed* to diagnose mental health disorders and provide psychotherapy; however, you are *not allowed* to prescribe medication.

These would be considered your professional boundaries, and you cannot operate outside of them no matter how skilled you may be.

To help you stay within your scope of practice, it's essential to develop clear, intentional language around how you integrate various approaches into your work; we will review some examples in just a minute. This, of course, will depend on your unique practice style, how you blend modalities, your areas of specialization, and your niche.

Additionally, your informed consent should include specific statements that clarify your role as a licensed behavioral health provider and emphasize that you are offering a single, unified clinical service—not multiple or separate services.

Let's review some examples.

"This is a clinical mental health practice. Any complementary or alternative tools offered are used solely to support and enhance psychotherapy—not to replace it."

"The complementary interventions I integrate—whether spiritual, energetic, or somatic—are always supplemental to the clinical work we are doing. They are not provided as stand-alone services and are only used when aligned with your treatment goals."

"These tools are integrated through the lens of my clinical practice framework and are only included when they complement your care and are appropriate within the therapeutic process."

"While some of the tools I use may also appear in coaching or wellness spaces, they are utilized here under a clinical lens, rooted in ethical standards and informed by psychological theory."

"You are never required to engage in any complementary or alternative practices. They are optional, always explained, and only used when it enhances—not substitutes—your therapeutic process."

Including statements like these in your informed consent, placing them on your website, and discussing them openly with clients, is essential for demonstrating that you are practicing within your legal and ethical scope. These statements clarify your role as a licensed mental health professional, affirm that psychotherapy is the primary service being delivered, and clearly communicate how any complementary or alternative tools are used in support of, not as a substitute for, clinical care.

By embedding this language into your documentation and conversations, you establish boundaries that protect both you and your clients, reinforce your clinical integrity, and ensure informed, collaborative decision-making. This isn't just about paperwork—it's about transparency, alignment, and honoring the standards of your profession while staying true to the integrative way you practice.

This transparency should also extend to your collaborative treatment plan—the one your client reviews and signs. It's your shared road map. If you're integrating complementary or spiritual practices, it's essential that your treatment goals reflect how those modalities support clinical progress. You and your client cocreate this plan, and every intervention used—whether it's somatic, intuitive, or energy-based—should clearly connect to those goals.

Dos and Don'ts when Integrating Spiritual and Energy-Based Practices in Clinical Practice

Reiki

Reiki is a form of energy healing that involves channeling universal life force energy to support emotional, physical, and energetic balance. In therapeutic settings, it is often used to help clients process or release somatic and emotional blockages that may not be accessible through cognitive methods alone.

Many of you have supported clients through deep psychoanalytic exploration of unconscious material, past experiences, and trauma. And in those moments, you may notice your own body start to respond—a tightening in your chest, a wave of nausea, a sense of collapse. This is known clinically as *somatic countertransference*. Some more spiritually attuned therapists may refer to this as *clairsentience*, the intuitive ability to feel another's emotional or energetic state through the body.

Do this . . .

Now, let's imagine that while your client can articulate the insight cognitively—"I realize now that I always had to take care of my mother emotionally"—they're still stuck. Their voice shakes, their hands tremble, and they clutch their chest as they say it. That's a signal that the nervous system is still holding something the mind alone can't release.

With consent, you might say, "It sounds like your body is still holding a lot here. Would it feel supportive if we paused and brought in some energy work to help your system release what it no longer needs to carry?"

You're not stopping the therapy—you're supporting it. You're using Reiki or another somatic/energetic intervention to meet the body where words can't reach. You're staying fully in your role as a therapist, using your tools *within* a regulated, intentional, and clinically informed container. You're still processing, documenting, and grounding the experience in the clinical goals and language of your work.

Don't do this . . .

Now let's flip this.

You should not have a client come in for a therapy session, say very little, lie on a table for a full sixty-minute hands-on Reiki treatment, and then document the session as psychotherapy. This crosses ethical boundaries, especially if there was no psychotherapeutic assessment, processing, or integration. In this case, you're not acting as a licensed mental health professional—you're functioning solely as a Reiki practitioner.

If you're billing insurance or presenting the session as clinical care, that becomes a scope of practice and transparency issue. It's not about the Reiki—it's about the lack of therapeutic engagement, documentation, link to treatment goals, and clearly defined roles.

Tarot/Oracle Cards

Tarot and oracle cards are a deck of cards known as reflective tools used to explore themes, emotions, and unconscious material through imagery and symbolism. In clinical work, they can support insight, metaphorical processing, and narrative development when facilitated through a client-centered, meaning-making lens.

Let's say you're supporting a client who's struggling to access their inner voice or make a difficult decision. You've explored their values, you've identified patterns rooted in family dynamics or attachment wounds, and yet . . . they're still circling. Cognitively, they understand the issue, but emotionally, they feel blocked or disconnected from their own wisdom.

Do this . . .

You might offer tarot or oracle cards not as a mystical solution but as a therapeutic tool, a creative and symbolic way to bypass cognitive defenses and help the client project meaning. Not to predict the future or override clinical reasoning but to externalize inner narratives and offer symbolic imagery that helps the client connect to unconscious material.

As the therapist, you're not offering "answers"; you're facilitating meaning-making.

Maybe a card's imagery speaks to something unspoken, and it opens up a new conversation: "This card is about transformation—how does that resonate with where you are right now?"

Suddenly, the conversation moves from stuck to symbolic, inviting depth, intuition, and creativity into the room. That's not outside the therapeutic process—that *is* the therapeutic process, using metaphor and reflection as clinically supported tools.

The card isn't the answer; it's the doorway. It's a coregulated, collaborative way to help the client access inner material, activate intuition, and explore options. You're not assigning fate or future outcomes. You're facilitating insight, deepening metaphor, and honoring the way your client makes meaning. When done well, it looks more like narrative therapy meets depth psychology than anything you'd find at a psychic fair. And again, you're documenting the clinical intention behind using the cards, just like you would with any experiential technique.

Again, let's flip this.

Don't do this . . .

You should not pull cards for a client, deliver an interpretation as truth or prediction, and base clinical decisions or treatment planning solely on what the cards say. That moves the work from reflective exploration into prescriptive authority—which strips the client of agency and fails to meet clinical standards. Tarot and oracle cards should not be used to bypass therapeutic dialogue, override clinical judgment, or introduce deterministic beliefs into the room. When you position the cards as "the answer" rather than a tool for cocreating meaning-making, you're no longer practicing therapy—you're providing a spiritual reading.

Crystals

Crystals are naturally occurring mineral formations often used in spiritual and energy-based practices to support intention-setting, grounding, emotional balance, and energetic alignment. In clinical work, they can serve as tactile, symbolic, and anchoring tools when used with intention, consent, and therapeutic relevance.

Let's say you're working with a client who struggles with dissociation during sessions. They often "float" or check out when approaching emotionally intense material. You've been supporting their awareness of nervous system responses, grounding strategies, and psychoeducation around trauma and dissociation. Still, they're having difficulty staying present in their body.

Do this . . .

You might offer a grounding crystal—such as hematite, smoky quartz, or black tourmaline—as an anchor object to support somatic presence. With consent and explanation, you could say, "Sometimes having a grounding object to hold can support staying present when the emotions feel intense. Would you be open to trying something tactile that might help you stay connected to your body?"

This isn't about claiming the crystal itself is healing the trauma. It's about offering a coregulation tool. The crystal becomes a physical anchor—like a weighted object or fidget—helping the client stay rooted in the here and now while doing emotionally challenging work. It may also serve as a symbolic container: "This crystal represents your right to stay safe and grounded while exploring your story."

When used this way, the crystal is a *means* to facilitate therapeutic engagement, not a substitute for it. You're supporting nervous system regulation, increasing distress tolerance, and helping the client build resources that bridge the body and mind. You can document this clearly as a somatic grounding intervention with symbolic and sensory support through the use of crystals.

Don't do this . . .

You should not give your client a crystal, tell them it will "absorb negative energy" or "heal their trauma," and avoid or bypass therapeutic processing. You should not make unfounded medical or psychological claims about the crystal's properties, especially if you're presenting the session as clinical therapy.

Similarly, you shouldn't hand a client a crystal without context and hope it does the work for you. That lacks intentionality, transparency, and clinical alignment. If you're treating the crystal as the healer and not offering a therapeutic frame or processing, you're stepping into unregulated spiritual work—not therapy.

Why does this matter? Because even something as seemingly benign as a rock can become ethically complex when used in the therapy room without clear clinical reasoning, documentation, and theoretical alignment.

Crystals aren't inherently clinical tools. But *you* are the clinician—and with proper training, intention, and scope clarity, you can ethically integrate them into trauma work, narrative therapy, somatic awareness, or symbolic processing that enriches your clinical process.

So why am I pressing this issue of integration so hard? Because I want you to stay firmly within your legally defined scope of practice. The moment you begin toggling between roles—one day showing up as a Reiki practitioner or spiritual healer, the next as a mental health therapist—you risk crossing professional boundaries. And that's not just semantics. That shift in role perception could be interpreted as delivering services that fall below your professional standards or outside your regulated scope of practice.

When that happens, you open yourself up to serious consequences: potential board investigation, accusations of unprofessional conduct, license suspension or revocation, and even malpractice liability. This is exactly what we're trying to avoid.

The most effective way to protect yourself is by making sure you are fully trained in any healing modality you integrate—this speaks to competency. You need to clearly articulate why you're using it, how it aligns with your clinical framework, what theoretical lens supports it, what treatment goal it supports, and what the potential benefits, risks, and research say about it.

But let me be clear: This is a razor-thin line. Integration isn't something you do passively or halfheartedly. It takes intentionality, clinical clarity, and full awareness of your role.

If you can't confidently explain how your approach serves a clinical purpose within your therapeutic scope, you're leaving yourself—and your license—wide open to scrutiny.

Now, I know some of you are probably thinking, *Okay, Tina, this all sounds great, but I can only do this if I'm in private practice and not billing insurance.*

That's not exactly what I'm saying. Because remember, you're not replacing psychotherapy with something else; you're expanding it. You're offering a holistic framework as a licensed behavioral health clinician.

And then there's the line I hear all the time: "But the insurance company will only reimburse me if I use evidence-based practices."

Okay, but let's get really clear—do you really mean evidence-based practices? Because that you can absolutely claim.

Or do you mean empirically supported treatment modalities? Because even if that's what's written in your contracts with insurances companies (and honestly, I haven't seen one of these contracts firsthand since providers are reluctant and limited in their ability to share the context of these documents and I do not take insurance), that doesn't mean you can't use complementary and alternative interventions to enhance those ESTs.

I train therapists every week on how to integrate Reiki, tarot, human design, somatic experiencing—you name it—with things like IFS, DBT, EMDR. It can be done. And when it's done well, you don't have to "lie" in your psychotherapy notes.

That's exactly why my colleague Vanessa Holliman, LCSW, and I created The Art of Integrative Documentation—a continuing education approved training that literally walks you through how to do this step by step. Informed consent, treatment goals, psychotherapy notes—the whole golden thread.

Because integration isn't about hiding what you do; it's about documenting it so clearly and ethically that no one can question it. If you are interested, more information is available for you on my website.

Competency

Competency is not the same as scope of practice—it's a crucial second layer. Even if your license allows you to *do* something, you shouldn't actually do it unless you are trained to do it *well*.

When I say "competent," I mean that you've developed the skills and understanding required to ethically apply a specific intervention in the clinical setting. Competency is defined by your formal education, supervised experience, continuing education, certifications, and even lived experience—but only if that lived experience has been meaningfully integrated into your ability to support others.

Think of it like this: As licensed therapists, we're all *permitted* to use cognitive behavioral therapy (CBT). But if you've never received formal training or supervision in it, you're not competent to use it yet.

The same applies to EMDR, DBT, ACT—and yes, to breathwork, energy healing, oracle cards, or intuitive development. Personal experience matters, but it's not enough. You need to be intentional about developing the skill set required to hold space for others using that tool.

Competency is your responsibility. If you're introducing unconventional tools into your practice, ask yourself the following:

What formal or structured training do I have?
Have I received feedback, consultation, or mentorship?
Can I describe this intervention clearly and ethically?
Does my training match the depth of how I plan to use it?

If you can't answer yes to those questions yet, it's not a no—it just means there's more work to do before you integrate it into your therapy space. Remember, there are rules to follow and expectations to demonstrate when you are working under a regulatory body.

So, we are back to this question: *How do I make sure my training is sufficient enough in the eyes of my professional and national boards?*

Now, I would define competency as this: the demonstrated ability to effectively and ethically deliver services based on sufficient knowledge, skill, training, and experience.

It reflects an integration of formal education, supervised practice, ongoing learning, and the capacity to apply interventions appropriately within one's scope of practice and client population.

But who cares what I think . . . let's look at what is written in black and white.

NASW Code of Ethics (2021), Section 1.04 – Competence:

> (a) Social workers should provide services and represent themselves as competent only within the boundaries of their education, training, license, certification, consultation received, supervised experience, or other relevant professional experience.

APA Code of Ethics (2017), Standard 2.01 – Boundaries of Competence:

> Psychologists provide services, teach, and conduct research with populations and in areas only within the boundaries of their competence, based on their education, training, supervised experience, consultation, study, or professional experience.

ACA Code of Ethics (2014), Section C.2.a – Boundaries of Competence:

> Counselors practice only within the boundaries of their competence, based on their education, training, supervised experience, state and national professional credentials, and appropriate professional experience.

AAMFT Code of Ethics (2015), Professional Competence and Integrity:

> Marriage and family therapists maintain high standards of professional competence. They provide services only within the boundaries of their competence, based on their education, training, supervised experience, and appropriate professional experience.

So, is competency a checkbox? Legally, sometimes, yes.

Now, you will also have to cross-reference this with your state statutes, laws, and admin codes. Most will follow the expectations laid out in a specific code of ethics, and others will not. Depending on your state, a three-hour online training might technically meet the minimum standard.

But ethically? Competency should always mean more than that. Especially when it comes to practices like Reiki, somatic work, or intuitive development, where the path to mastery often includes personal practice, lineage respect, and embodied skill—not just a certificate. So yes, check the box. *And* also hold yourself to a higher standard.

Remember, competency is both a document you can show your board and a commitment you make to your clients—to ensure what you're offering is grounded, integrated, and delivered with clarity, safety, and care. That's the bar we set here. And that's how we protect our clients and our integrity.

Dual Relationships

Let's also talk about dual relationships, because there are a lot of misconceptions floating around.

Most professional boards define a dual relationship as any relationship that extends beyond the therapeutic context and could impair your objectivity, competence, or create a risk of exploitation or harm to your client.

But here's the thing: Each licensing board and code of ethics has its own take on this. Some explicitly prohibit dual relationships no matter the circumstances. Others allow some flexibility—but only if you can prove that your objectivity remains intact and that the client is not being harmed or coerced in any way.

The reason this issue is taken so seriously? Because objectivity and power dynamics are slippery.

Clearly, they're slippery—otherwise, we wouldn't need entire ethics sections reminding people of this little gem: Don't sleep with your clients.

Like . . . seriously.

At this point, if you still need a reminder, maybe therapy isn't the field for you.

You may feel confident that you're not exploiting anyone or that your roles are clear in your own mind—but that's not enough. The burden of proof is on you to demonstrate that your client understands the boundaries, gave informed consent, and is not at risk for harm or confusion.

And that's why some boards and codes don't leave much room for interpretation. In their eyes, the potential for exploitation is baked into the overlap, and that's reason enough to prohibit the relationship.

Now, if you're exploring coaching as a separate service—great. I'm not here to stop you. If you want to legally separate your practices and offer coaching outside therapy, go for it. That's just not what I'm teaching here.

And more importantly: Even when you're operating under a different title, your license still follows you.

You're still bound by the ethical and legal expectations of your professional role. That means things like mandated reporting, scope of practice, and transparency about limitations and risks still apply.

So, if you're blending spiritual or complementary services into therapy—or moving clients between coaching and therapy roles, or combining them in the same spiritual group—you can't fall back on "but I wasn't trying to harm anyone" or "I can stay objective." That's not enough. These situations can get ethically murky fast. You need clear documentation, theory-based justification, and fully informed consent to back it up—*before* the lines get blurry.

As always, let's look through some examples . . .

From a NASW Code of Ethics (2021), Section 1.06(c):

> Social workers should avoid dual or multiple relation-
> ships with clients or former clients in which there is
> a risk of exploitation or potential harm to the client.

This means that any relationship, personal, financial, or otherwise, that might impair professional judgment, increase the risk of harm, or lead to blurred boundaries, should be carefully evaluated and often avoided. The key factor is risk, not simply the existence of another relationship.

From the APA Code of Ethics – Standard 3.05 Multiple Relationships:

> A multiple relationship exists when a psychologist is in a professional role with a person and . . . at the same time is in another role with the same person.

The APA adds that these dual relationships must be avoided if they could reasonably be expected to impair objectivity, competence, or effectiveness in performing professional duties.

From California Board of Behavioral Sciences (BBS) – Dual Relationships:

> A situation where, in addition to the professional relationship, the therapist has another significant personal, financial, or professional relationship with the client or a close associate of the client.

They go on to explain that while not all dual relationships are inherently unethical, the therapist must ensure that the secondary relationship does not impair objectivity or effectiveness, or risk exploitation.

New York State Education Department for Licensed Mental Health Practitioners (NYCRR § 52.32–33):

> You should recognize and avoid the dangers of dual relationships when relating to patients in more than one context, whether professional, social, educational, or commercial. Dual relationships can occur simultaneously or consecutively.

Examples include treating someone you're related to, socializing with clients, bartering, or having any business relationship with them.

So, as regulations vary, the consistency is that if it risks your objectivity or the client's welfare, it's a no-go, as multiple roles with a client, even unintentional, may cross ethical lines.

That's why we—say it with me—read our state laws, rules, codes, and national boards! Please—I beg of you—pull up your regulations and get familiar with how your license defines dual relationships. This isn't about fear. It's about power. The more you know, the more confidently you can practice with integrity, especially when you're doing something that pushes the norms.

(*cue that old NBC PSA star shooting across the screen*)

Let's end this chapter with something I really want you to hear loud and clear.

How You Advertise Yourself Matters

I've worked with so many therapists who've trained in modalities like past-life regression, Emotion Code, Body Code, Belief Code, ancestral healing, integrative energy practices, Reiki, astrology, angel card readings, spinal energetics, HeartMath, mediumship, nutrition, quantum healing, shamanic practices, sound healing, breathwork—you name it, I've seen it. And honestly? It's been incredible. I've learned so much just by witnessing what's out there.

But here's the thing: Most of these certifications and trainings don't come from licensed mental health professionals. They come from gifted, seasoned practitioners—people who deeply embody their work and pass it on with integrity. But their job is to teach the modality, *not* to help you ethically integrate it into a therapy practice under licensure.

So what happens? Therapists take these trainings, experience profound personal healing, fall in love with the work, and want to bring it to their clients—because they see what's possible when we pair energetic and spiritual healing with the depth of psychotherapy. They feel the pull. The alignment. The expansion. But then they hit the wall of "how the hell do I do this without risking my license?"

That's where I come in. That's what this entire framework is for.

But here's one of the most common pitfalls I see: Those shiny certifications often come with shiny new titles—Energy Practitioner, Reiki Master, Quantum Healer, Intuitive Guide, Embodiment Coach. And listen, I get the excitement. These titles feel powerful and meaningful. You earned them.

But when you are integrating these practices *into* clinical work, you are not showing up as those titles. You are showing up first and foremost as a licensed mental health professional—a psychotherapist, social worker, counselor, or marriage and family therapist. That's the role under which you're legally practicing. You can absolutely share that you've trained in Reiki or studied ancestral healing or learned tarot—but you are not marketing yourself as a Reiki Master Therapist or a Quantum Intuitive Counselor or any hybrid identity that muddies the waters.

Why does this matter?

Because titles create expectations. What you advertise on your website can be used as a legal document. They tell the public—and your licensing board—what kind of service you're offering. And if your website or *Psychology Today* says "Spiritual Energy Healer," but you're billing insurance as a mental health therapist? That opens the door to confusion, scrutiny, and serious ethical questions about scope of practice. And let me ask you, are you ready to answer that?

So no, I'm not saying you have to hide your certifications or throw away the titles that feel meaningful to you. What I *am* saying is that when you are working under your clinical license, you must lead with your clinical title. Your role is clear. Your lane is defined. Your integration is intentional.

And that clarity? It protects your license, your clients, and your integrity.

I Lied ... There's One More Thing You Need to Know

Some of the modalities you're trained in—like massage therapy, acupuncture, or nutrition—might actually be regulated professions in your state, governed by entirely separate boards with their own licensing requirements, scope of practice rules, and legal protections. That means if you start practicing those modalities without proper licensure (even if you're doing it "within therapy"), you could be violating state law and crossing into another profession's jurisdiction.

This opens up a whole new can of compliance.

Are you using a modality that's regulated in your state?

Are you claiming a title that's protected by law?

Are there specific informed consent or disclosure requirements for that practice?

So please, add this to your must-do list: check whether your state has a regulatory board for the modality you're trained in. Read their rules. Make sure your clinical work isn't in conflict with their expectations. Integration doesn't mean blending everything into a legal gray area—it means respecting the boundaries of each lane so you don't end up in a legal mess.

When in doubt? Clarity and compliance are your best friends.

Chapter 5
The Link—Theory Without the Textbook Chains

When I first started diving deep into the legal and ethical side of integrating complementary and alternative interventions, one thing stood out over and over again: the repeated emphasis on *clinical theory*.

As I combed through state laws, licensing board statutes, and codes of ethics across disciplines—social work, marriage and family therapy, counseling—the language I saw wasn't about modalities. As we have already reviewed, it wasn't about specific techniques or even evidence-based treatments. What kept surfacing was the importance of grounding your work in theoretical principles, concepts, and values.

This was a lightbulb moment for me.

So many of us are asking, *How do I justify this healing modality in my therapy practice?*

And the answer is this: through theoretical alignment.

I need to be honest with you: I used to be terrified of clinical theory. The very idea of it made me shut down. And looking back, I know exactly why.

When I was in my master's program at New York University, I had a professor in my human behavior class who just did *not* enjoy my questions—especially when I pushed back on having to pick a single diagnosis or when I couldn't easily land on one modality or theoretical framework. I genuinely saw merit in multiple approaches. I wasn't trying to be difficult—I was trying to be thorough, to understand the differences. But that curiosity wasn't welcomed.

And this was a million years ago, when if you wanted your grade back early, you had to print your paper, hand it in with a self-addressed, stamped envelope, and then wait for it to be mailed back to you before the summer ended.

So, when my paper finally arrived in the mail, I tore open the envelope—and inside was a C–. Wild, right? I got a C– in a graduate program, even worse an NYU graduate program! But it didn't stop there. There was also a handwritten note left for me on my paper: "I think it's time that you make the decision to leave the program. You're not grasping these concepts."

Attention All Current Master's-Level Students

If you've ever been shut down, dismissed, or made to feel small in your graduate program for asking bold questions or thinking differently—this is your reminder: That's not okay.

A professor should never speak at you without curiosity, without conversation, without a moment of pause to ask why something mattered to you. If they drop a comment that makes you shrink instead of expand—that's not mentorship. That's misalignment with the very values this field claims to uphold.

> I didn't have the words at the time to speak up for myself—but I found them later. You will too. And I promise you: Staying curious, thinking critically, and coloring outside the lines does not make you a bad clinician. It makes you a powerful one. Don't let their fear shrink your fire.

I remember reading that and whispering, "Fuck you," to the professor who will not be named. Then I ripped the paper to shreds and threw it out. But I didn't speak up again after that. I kept my head down. I stopped challenging. I played the game. And what that moment taught me—unfortunately—was that curiosity and critical thinking might actually hurt me in this field. So I shut it off.

After that, I stopped engaging with theory altogether. I became the therapist who, when someone asked what framework I used, would say, "CBT." Because that's what the "good" therapists said. That answer was safe. It wouldn't raise eyebrows. No one would question it. But the truth? I didn't connect to CBT. I just didn't want to feel stupid again.

When I went back for my doctorate in social work thirteen years after that soul-crushing NYU experience, I knew there was a theory course waiting for me—and honestly, I was dreading it. All those old wounds came rushing back: the fear of saying the wrong thing, of being too much, of not being enough. But that all changed when I met Dr. Manny González.

Dr. González didn't just teach theory; he saw the beauty in it. He loved the story behind each framework just as much as he loved the stories inside each of us as students. He helped us see theory not as a dry requirement but as a living, breathing reflection of how we understand healing. He helped me understand that theory is not about picking a box and squeezing into it—it's about giving our work a foundation, a backbone, a *why*.

Especially in research, theory justifies the purpose. It helps you explain why your work matters. And that changed everything for me. The theory that aligned most with my dissertation was integrative body-mind-spirit social work, developed by Mo Yee Lee, Cecilia Chan, Siu-Man Ng, and Pamela Leung. This framework emphasizes holistic healing that not only is grounded in mind-body connection but also honors the cultural, spiritual, and energetic dimensions of human experience. It gave language and legitimacy to what I knew deep in my bones: Healing is multifaceted, and our clinical frameworks must reflect that.

At the same time, another professor—Dr. Morgan Cooley—assigned us a paper on our personal "theory of change." That one hit different. It invited me to pause, look inward, and reflect:

How do I believe people change?
Why do I work the way I do?

And that question didn't lead me to textbooks. It led me straight back to my own story—my transformation, my survival, my healing, my reckoning with spirituality, identity, and voice.

I started naming the pieces of my journey that shaped me—especially my "toxic phase," the breakdowns that cracked me open, and the sacred, soul-deep strategies I used to piece myself back together. I realized: My story was already rooted in theory. I just hadn't had the language or made the connection yet.

Transpersonal and Jungian psychology showed up in how I understood my purpose as part of something much bigger than this dimension. I had to explore unconscious patterns, inherited narratives, and spiritual symbolism to discover who

I was. I dove deep into shadow work and inner child healing—not just to analyze my pain but to *honor* it.

I began to see that my role on this planet wasn't a fluke. It was divinely designed. My spiritual connection, my intuitive knowing, my sense of being part of a larger collective—these weren't random; they were *transpersonal truths.*

Psychodynamic theory helped me name the inner belief systems I carried, both from my past and my lineage. It helped me trace patterns, loops, and coping mechanisms that once kept me "safe" and now needed to be reworked. Defense mechanisms, attachment wounds—these weren't abstract ideas. They were living parts of my story that I had to confront and renegotiate.

Existential-humanistic and person-centered frameworks helped me reclaim my right to choose. To define who I was beyond what my family or the field expected of me. To step into my Black Sheep identity with pride—not shame. These frameworks gave me the permission to say, "I matter. My truth matters. My way of practicing is valid—even if it doesn't look like anyone else's."

This internal reckoning—the process of naming, claiming, and integrating my own beliefs—became the foundation for how I now show up with my clients. As a therapist, I don't force people into boxes. I honor their wholeness, their contradictions, their wounds and wisdom. I listen to what's spoken and unspoken. I track the energetic, the emotional, the spiritual, and the clinical all at once. I help them explore what keeps them stuck and guide them back into a relationship with their *self*—not by imposing an agenda but by offering a deeply attuned, collaborative process of becoming.

And as a coach, I hold space for other Black Sheep therapists to do the same. I help them reclaim their power, find their voice, and ground their magic in clinical theory so they can practice with integrity *and* freedom. I don't teach people how to be me—I teach them how to become fully themselves. When you bring language to it, when you claim it with clarity and courage, you create a practice that no one else could ever replicate.

The theories that once made me feel like an outsider are now the very frameworks that give me—and the people I serve—permission to thrive.

Theory vs. Modalities

Theory is a structured framework that explains how and why psychological change occurs. It helps us understand what causes suffering, what influences behavior, and what supports healing.

According to Gerald Corey (2017), theory provides the road map that guides clinicians in choosing interventions, understanding the therapeutic relationship, and making sense of the client's story.

But here's the thing: When I started asking therapists to tell me what theories guide their practice—what beliefs or frameworks shape the way they work—I kept getting hit with modalities.

"I use EMDR."

"I'm trained in DBT."

"I love using acceptance and commitment therapy."

While those are valuable tools, they're not theories. They're modalities and approaches—but they don't explain *why* change happens, just *how* to apply certain interventions to create change.

And I get it—because I used to be the same way. Most of us weren't actually taught this stuff in depth. While state laws, licensing boards, and codes of ethics reference clinical theory over and over again as the foundation of ethical, competent care, many graduate programs breeze past it. The focus instead tends to be on evidence-based practices or empirically supported treatments—despite the fact that those terms rarely appear in the actual statutes or ethical codes that govern our licenses (what is that about?).

Theory, somehow, didn't get the same spotlight. It's not emphasized as a learning competency the way modalities are, and it's definitely not something you'll see trending on Instagram or TikTok. I mean not yet . . . Go follow me @the_blacksheep_therapist on IG and @theblacksheeptherapist on TikTok!

Even in clinical trainings, many facilitators skip over the theoretical underpinnings and go straight to the application—maybe because they themselves don't feel grounded in it?

But here's the problem: When you skip the theory, you lose the *why*.

You lose the ability to confidently explain why something works, when it's appropriate to use it, and how it is beneficial in the therapy room. And that's when impostor syndrome creeps in.

So here's what I want you to know: Theory gives you power.

It is the belief system behind your process. It's not just the foundation of your interventions—it's the anchor for how you move, how you make decisions, and how you justify the integration of any modality into your clinical work.

In contrast, modalities are the tools, strategies, or interventions you use in the therapy room. These include things like EMDR, DBT, ACT, CBT, mindfulness, narrative therapy, or Reiki and breathwork. Modalities are the *how*, interventions are the *what*—but theory is *why* you do them.

The Theory Behind the Modality

Every clinical modality has an underlying theory or conceptual lens that supports its application and explains why it works.

Eye Movement Desensitization and Reprocessing (EMDR)

Take EMDR, for example—a modality developed by Francine Shapiro (2001, 2017). One of its central theoretical foundations is adaptive information processing (AIP) theory, which suggests the brain has a natural drive toward psychological healing, organizing experiences into adaptive memory networks. But when trauma overwhelms this system, the memory doesn't get properly processed. It gets "stuck" in a maladaptive form—locked in the nervous system with the original images, emotions, beliefs, and body sensations still intact.

AIP views symptoms like anxiety, shame, or hypervigilance not as isolated problems but as signs of unresolved memories still "running" in the background. EMDR activates the brain's innate capacity to complete that disrupted processing. Through bilateral stimulation and targeted recall, it helps the brain access the stuck memory network and reintegrate it into a broader adaptive system—where the emotional charge softens, the story shifts, and the client no longer feels hijacked by the past. That's the AIP mechanism in action: trauma resolution through reprocessing, not just desensitization.

Dialectic Behavioral Therapy (DBT)

DBT, developed by Dr. Marsha Linehan (1993, 2015), is grounded in biosocial theory—a framework that explains emotional dysregulation as the result of a person's biological sensitivity interacting with an invalidating environment. Some individuals are born with a heightened emotional baseline: They feel things more intensely, return to equilibrium more slowly, and experience a deeper internal response to stress or pain. When these emotional cues are consistently dismissed, punished, or misunderstood, particularly by early caregivers, it can lead to chronic self-doubt, shame, and difficulty regulating emotions.

DBT addresses this by offering a therapeutic space that is both validating and skills-based. Clients learn concrete tools, like mindfulness, distress tolerance, emotion regulation, and interpersonal effectiveness, to navigate overwhelming emotional states. Just as importantly, the therapy relationship itself becomes a corrective emotional experience—one where validation is consistent, earned trust is modeled, and emotional responses are honored, not pathologized. This dual focus helps reshape the client's internal narrative: Emotions are real, they are survivable, and they can be managed with clarity and confidence. That's the core of biosocial theory in action—healing the damage of invalidation while building the skills needed for long-term emotional resilience.

Acceptance and Commitment Therapy (ACT)

We can even see this in ACT, created by Dr. Steven C. Hayes. This modality is grounded in relational frame theory (RFT), which explains how humans naturally develop complex language and cognition by linking words and concepts through learned relationships (Hayes, Barnes-Holmes, and Roche 2001). But this powerful ability to make meaning also creates suffering—because the mind doesn't just describe experiences; it evaluates, judges, and predicts them based on past associations. For example, someone who's learned to associate "failure" with "worthlessness" might avoid challenges not because they're dangerous but because the meaning attached to them feels intolerable.

ACT supports change by helping clients step out of these rigid cognitive frames (Hayes, Strosahl, and Wilson 1999). Through mindfulness, acceptance, and values-based action, clients learn to observe thoughts without being dominated by them. Instead of arguing with the mind, they build psychological flexibility—making space for discomfort, clarifying what matters, and choosing actions that align with their values. In this way, RFT isn't just a theory of language—it's a blueprint for transformation. ACT helps clients rewrite their relationship with suffering, not by eliminating pain but by shifting how they relate to it.

You're Ready to Discover Your Framework—Now What?

If I've officially convinced you to jump on the theory train, the next question I usually get is, "How the hell do I know what theory aligns with how I practice or with my story?"

And honestly? I don't believe in giving people a long list of theories and saying, "Pick which one feels right." Because the truth is, if you read a well-written theoretical framework, you'll find something in it that resonates. Most therapists will. But that doesn't mean it reflects the *essence* of who you are, how you practice, or how you see change unfold in the room.

The question isn't just, What sounds nice?

It's, What theory explains your own healing process? What framework describes how you believe people grow, change, and transform? What ideas do you want to emphasize and share with clients as part of your therapeutic presence?

And let me just say this while we're here: If schools are still telling therapists to leave their belief systems at the door, that's wild to me.

No, we should not be shoving our beliefs down clients' throats.

But pretending that therapists don't have belief systems is straight-up crazy.

In fact, your beliefs about how people heal and grow are essential to how you practice.

They inform your treatment planning, your choice of modalities, and your relational style. They should be transparent to your clients so clients can choose if your approach fits their preferences and values.

Let's revisit the evidence-based practice framework we talked about earlier—remember, one of the core pillars is the alignment with clients' preferences and values.

How can a client know whether your approach aligns with their values if you can't even speak on it?

Let me be blunt: If you can't articulate the *why* behind what you do, if you don't know how change happens in your presence, or what clients might expect from your approach—you're not practicing in alignment with evidence-based care.

And yes, I'll go as far as saying that *can* make you a dangerous therapist. Not because you don't care but because you're lacking clarity—and that's where lack of attunement and harm can happen.

I can say this because I *was* that therapist. And this isn't about shame—it's about power. In this next section, I will walk you through a step-by-step guide on not only how to identify the theories that influence your practice but also how to build an Integrative Clinical Practice Framework that speaks to your practice style.

CHAPTER 6
YOUR STORY MATTERS—AND IT'S THE KEY TO YOUR FREEDOM

Once you begin to understand that theory isn't just academic fluff but actually the language of your deepest knowledge and applications, you can begin to own it. That's where this next part comes in.

I created a process called the Soul Purpose Masterplan—a reverse-engineered reflection designed to uncover the roots of your practice. It's not about memorizing theories or squeezing yourself into someone else's framework. It's about helping you see that you've already been practicing from a theoretical lens—you just haven't had the words for it yet.

This process helps you identify and create your Integrative Clinical Practice Framework, which becomes the foundation for explaining how you practice. It's how you articulate who you are, how you work, what you believe, and how you support change. It's what helps your ideal clients say, "Ohhh, that's the therapist I've been looking for."

Here's how we begin.

Your Personal Story

The first phase of this process is all about reflection. I walk therapists through a set of structured journal prompts that tap into the layers of their lived experience—not just the clinical stuff but the personal wisdom they've gained from their own healing journey.

This isn't surface level. This is deep. Messy. Beautiful. Honest. I'm not gonna lie, most therapists have gotten triggered. And my response to that: Good, we are cracking something open!

Before we dive in, here's the thing: Some questions open us up right away. Others need to be asked in three different ways before the answer clicks. That's why you'll see questions here that circle around the same ideas from different angles. This isn't about "getting it right"—it's about getting honest.

Use these questions to spark your reflection. Write what comes, leave what doesn't. The examples aren't here to box you in; they're here to show you the range of what's possible.

The Core Questions

1. What aspects of your upbringing, identity, or worldview shape who you are today?
2. What pivotal experiences shaped how you understand people, pain, and healing?
3. What cracked you open—the events you wouldn't choose again but wouldn't undo either?
4. Which practices or experiences helped you feel like yourself again (or for the first time)?
5. What roles, wounds, or lessons keep showing up in your life?

6. How do your values, turning points, tools, and lessons weave into a single story of who you are as a person?

Now let's dive deeper into each question.

Pro Tip: If you recall, in the introduction of this book, I gifted you a complimentary guide to assist you in your theory identification journey. This would be a great time to download your free copy of *From Magic to Method: The Black Sheep Therapist Theory Compass* to use alongside the next three chapters. You can access it by scanning the QR code.

Question 1: Which aspects of your upbringing, identity, or worldview shape who you are today?

Theories don't just live in textbooks—they often live in us, long before we know their names. This first step helps surface the values, assumptions, and worldview that quietly shape our entire approach to healing.

Here are some sample answers:

- I grew up in a military family where emotions were "handled privately." That gave me a deep respect for privacy—but also a drive to create spaces where feelings can be spoken out loud.
- Being the eldest child in an immigrant household taught me responsibility early but also made me the family translator and fixer—roles I still notice myself taking with clients.

- As a queer teen in a conservative town, I learned to code-switch for safety. Now I see masking as a survival skill and help clients unlearn it when it's no longer needed.

Question 2: What pivotal experiences shaped how you understand people, pain, and healing?

Life experience shapes the way you "feel" a room, not just how you think about it. It's the invisible curriculum behind your clinical instincts. These moments become the emotional palette from which you now work. It can reveal why certain client stories hit you harder, why you instinctively pause or lean in, and why you hold space the way you do.

Here are some sample answers:

- A devastating breakup in my twenties taught me that grief can be disorienting and sacred at the same time.
- Watching my parent recover from a life-threatening illness taught me how resilience often comes from small, daily acts of hope.
- Volunteering in a domestic violence shelter in college completely reshaped my understanding of safety and trust.

Question 3: What cracked you open—the events you wouldn't choose again but wouldn't undo either?

Big shifts are more than personal upheavals—they're initiations. They don't just change your life; they shift your framework for how you experience life. In this step, you begin to uncover the real reason you're drawn to certain theories, practices, or client struggles—because you've *lived* them.

Here are some sample answers:

- Burnout landed me in the ER, and I realized self-abandonment was the root cause.
- A spiritual awakening during my own therapy challenged every belief I had about change and healing.
- Leaving a toxic job showed me that my worth is not tied to productivity.

Question 4: Which practices or experiences helped you feel like yourself again (or for the first time)?

Each practice you turn to carries its own worldview about change, healing, and human nature. That worldview often aligns with a theory you didn't know you were already living.

Something I've seen time and time again with therapists who want to bring spiritual and energy-based modalities into clinical work: embodiment. They utilize these practices, daily, and are modeling what they want to teach to their clients.

This is similar to a promise I have always made to my clients: If I haven't used it, I'm not bringing it into the therapy room.

Here are some sample answers:

- Somatic experiencing taught me how to come back to my body when my mind was spiraling.
- Tarot helped me name patterns I didn't yet have language for.
- Reiki gave me a sense of calm I couldn't find in talk therapy alone.

Question 5: What roles, wounds, or lessons keep showing up in your life?

The roles and emotional patterns you've carried throughout your life often reveal the deeper psychology behind how you relate, how you help, and how you heal. When you name the archetypes you embody—like advocate, nurturer, guide, or alchemist—you're also naming the therapeutic stance you naturally take. These themes offer clues about your theoretical orientation, whether you realize it or not.

Here are some sample answers:

- I've always been the one people turn to in a crisis—and I've learned to hold that role with healthier boundaries.
- Abandonment themes have shown up in every stage of my life, which makes me deeply attuned to clients' fears of loss.
- I often play the role of translator—between cultures, between emotions, between worlds—and I now see that as a gift in my work.

Question 6: How do your values, turning points, tools, and lessons weave into a single story of who you are as a person?

This is the moment your story becomes your clinical framework. Your narrative becomes the ethical and intuitive compass for how you practice. It gives structure to your instincts, language to your intuition, and integrity to your integration. This is where your lived wisdom meets clinical legitimacy—and that's what makes your work not only effective but transformative.

Here are some sample answers:

- I used to see my sensitivity as weakness, but now I know it's my source of connection and strength.
- Losing what I thought defined me made me discover the parts of myself I'd ignored.

- I've learned that growth isn't about becoming someone new—it's about remembering who I've always been.

Seeing the Story Through a Theoretical Lens

Now, this part of the process is where I come in—and honestly, it's one of my favorite parts. It's a lot easier for me to do this work with others because I'm not emotionally attached to their story. I get to look at it with fresh, objective eyes—just like you do when you sit with a client and gently reflect something back to them that they hadn't noticed before.

That moment when a client says, "I've never thought about it that way," is the same magic that happens when I get to reflect a therapist's story back through the lens of theory.

At this point in the process, I usually start identifying multiple clinical theories that are most present in a therapist's journey—and then highlight exactly where I see those theories showing up in their story, language, and lived experience. For simplicity purposes, I will only be reviewing one theoretical framework in the example below, but my feedback typically includes between five and ten theories.

Jill's Story

Let me introduce you to someone I'll call "Jill." Like many of the therapists I work with, Jill came to me midcareer. She was a licensed marriage and family therapist in California with an established private practice. From the outside, things looked solid—steady referrals, clients who paid, a calendar that was rarely empty. But inside, Jill felt stuck. Despite having built something "successful," she was deeply unfulfilled.

What she really wanted was to bring her "whole damn self" into the room. Over the years, Jill had been on a powerful healing journey of her own—exploring energy work, deepening her spiritual practice, and reconnecting with nature. She told me that she dreamed of integrating Reiki, intuitive development, crystal healing, and breathwork into her therapy sessions. She imagined weaving in somatic practices inspired by being outdoors—movement, grounding techniques, even sessions on the beach. These weren't passing curiosities; they were practices that had transformed her personally, ones she had embodied. But every time she brought up these ideas in consultation, she was met with confusion, dismissal, or the same vague suggestion: "Maybe you should just do coaching."

And that didn't sit right.

Jill had worked too hard for her license, too long building her clinical practice, to walk away now. Coaching felt like a step sideways—or worse, a step down. She wasn't trying to leave therapy. She was trying to evolve it.

When I asked about her theoretical orientation, she paused. Then, almost whispering, she admitted she wasn't sure. She said she felt embarrassed not to have a clear answer—like maybe she had missed something critical in her training. But the truth is, Jill's experience is incredibly common. Most therapists aren't taught how to integrate who they are with what they do. They're trained to follow a manual, not write their own.

So that's where we began. Not with branding or niche development but with the core: who Jill was, what she believed about healing, and how those beliefs already lived quietly beneath her work.

After our first session, I gave Jill the same reflective worksheets I offer every therapist in my Innovative Practitioner Accelerator Program—structured prompts designed to peel back the layers of who you are, how you came to this work, and what you truly believe about healing. My favorite thing is when I get an email back that says, "I stopped overthinking and just started word dumping." That's when I know we're getting somewhere.

And Jill did exactly that.

I love those responses—the messy grammar, the curse words, the tangents. I love it when the professional mask comes off and what's left is the raw, unfiltered truth of a therapist finally telling the whole story. That kind of honesty? That's where the real work begins. Because inside that word dump is gold. Inside those messy sentences is the clarity they've been chasing.

That kind of vulnerability cracks something open—and in Jill's case, it was the doorway to ownership. Ownership of her story, her values, her perspectives. And once she let herself fully show up on the page, I got to do my favorite part: lean in with deep curiosity, gently tug on threads of her story, and reflect back the clinical alignment that was always there, just waiting to be named.

This process is never about perfection—it's about truth. And when a therapist shows up with that level of emotional investment and self-inquiry, I already know what kind of clinician they are. Jill's commitment to her own evolution, her willingness to look inward, to question, to write through the chaos—that told me everything. Because, as I've always said, the best clinicians model what they teach.

And what I saw in Jill was a powerhouse. A healer who just needed someone to help her make sense of her magic through a clinical lens.

And when I read through her responses, one line stopped me in my tracks. She described a moment on retreat where she heard, clear as day: *Feel your answer—don't think it.* That sentence alone told me we weren't just working with cognitive material. We were tapping into something deeper—something spiritual, intuitive, and energetically alive.

Jill's story was filled with these moments: ancestral dreams, energetic clearings, the first time she felt Reiki run through her hands, and the sense of "remembering" who she was, rather than learning something new. None of it could be explained away by behavioral theory. And none of it needed to be.

So I offered her a framework that could hold it.

I gently invited her to explore transpersonal psychology—a theory rooted in the understanding that healing is not limited to the individual mind but includes the soul, the sacred, and the unseen. Transpersonal theory makes room for intuition, for synchronicity, for inner knowing that doesn't always come from formal instruction. It aligns with the idea that transformation is not just psychological—it's also spiritual, ancestral, and energetic (Caplan, Hartelius, and Rardin 2003).

And as soon as she began reading into it, Jill lit up. Not because she had found a label but because she had finally found language for what she already knew to be true. That's the power of this work. When a theory reflects your lived experience back to you, it stops feeling like something you have to memorize—and starts becoming something you embody.

I took the language Jill naturally used to describe her transformation and reflected back how it aligned with the core principles of transpersonal psychology. No jargon. No stretching. Just revealing what was already there. This is what we mean when we say theory can amplify your clarity—not restrict it.

If you are thinking, *Okay, Tina, well, how do I know which theories align with my story?* Don't worry, I got you. Right now, your focus just needs to be on bringing your story to the surface. Trust me. Let's keep going—because this is where things really start to click.

Chapter 7
Owning Your Clinical Voice

Once we've explored your personal story and the themes that have shaped your inner transformation, the next part of the process is about how you show up as a professional.

I believe this part is critical. Because let's be honest—who you are in the room with clients isn't just shaped by what you learned in school. It's shaped by why you came into this field, how you've navigated it, and what you've come to believe about healing through your own lived experience *in* the profession.

When I'm working with therapists in my program, I ask them a series of questions that get to the heart of how their professional identity has formed and evolved. These reflections help uncover patterns and preferences that shape their clinical style, point us toward aligned theories, and highlight the unique magic they bring to the work—especially for those of us who never quite fit the mold.

Below are some of the core questions I use.

Ten Questions to Help You Discover Your Voice

1. What truly made you want to become a therapist or healing practitioner in the first place?

2. What helped you make that decision? What was the dream?

3. Why did you choose the specific discipline you entered—social work, psychology, counseling, marriage and family therapy? Was there something specific about that pillar that called to you?

4. What did you think this field would be like when you finished school? What assumptions did you hold about the work?

5. Once you started practicing, how different or similar was reality compared to those expectations?

6. Have you noticed any personal life patterns that have carried over into your professional life?

7. Are there emotional or relational themes from your past that show up again and again in the clinical space?

8. What makes your practice style unique or distinct? What have you learned through practice that school never taught you?

9. Are there any specific modalities, practices, or processes you consistently bring into your work? What themes or interventions keep reappearing in your sessions, no matter who you're working with?

10. Out of the theories I connected with your personal story, which ones resonated and why?

Now let's dive deeper into each question.

Question 1: What truly made you want to become a therapist or healing practitioner in the first place?

This first step grounds your entire professional framework in something real: *you*. Before licenses, certifications, or modalities there was a moment that called you to this work.

Reconnecting with that moment reminds you why you're here. It helps you separate your deeper purpose from the noise of professional expectations. When the field feels rigid or the path unclear, this origin story becomes your compass. It's not just sentimental—it's strategic. Because anchoring your clinical identity in something true and lived is the first step to building a practice that *feels like yours*.

Here's a sample answer:

> I remember sitting with a friend in college during a breakup and feeling completely present with her in her pain—no need to fix, just witness. She said, "You made me feel human again." That stuck with me. I didn't know it then, but that was the first time I understood what healing connection could look like.

Question 2: What helped you make that decision? What was the dream?

Your original dream may have been tender, idealistic, even a little naive—and that's okay. That vision held your *why* before the field taught you all its "rules." Revisiting it now doesn't mean you have to recreate it exactly—it means you get to honor the heartbeat behind it. The dream helps us name what truly matters to *you* in your work: safety, connection, meaning, presence. These aren't small things. They're the roots of how you define healing. When you remember what you were dreaming of, you start to see what your practice is missing—and what it's ready to reclaim.

Here's a sample answer:

> I imagined having a cozy office with warm lighting, helping people come back to themselves. I wanted to be the kind of person I never had growing up—some-

one safe, someone who really saw people.

Question 3: Why did you choose the specific discipline you entered—social work, psychology, counseling, marriage and family therapy? Was there something specific about that pillar that called to you?

The discipline you chose didn't just give you a license—it gave you a lens. Whether it was social justice, systemic thinking, relational dynamics, or a deep dive into the human psyche, your path shaped how you understand healing and change. Reconnecting with what originally called you to this pillar helps you reclaim your unique voice in the field. It reminds you that your discipline was never meant to limit you—it was meant to *ground* you. When you remember the values that drew you in, you can begin to align your practice with them again—on your own terms.

Here's a sample answer:

> I chose social work because it felt expansive—it made room for clinical work, community systems, and advocacy. I didn't want to feel boxed in. I've always been someone who sees the bigger picture, and social work felt like the only field that honored that.

Question 4: What did you think this field would be like when you finished school? What assumptions did you hold about the work?

The expectations we carry into our chosen field shape how we measure our success—and our disappointment. Naming the assumptions you once held helps you identify where the disillusionment started. It's not about blaming yourself for being idealistic; it's about honoring the version of you that truly believed in this work. That vision still matters. When you can separate the dream from the dysfunction, you start to see what's worth keeping—and what you're ready to rebuild.

Here's a sample answer:

> I thought I'd be doing deep, life-changing work every day—like peeling back emotional layers with clients who were ready to transform. Working with my perfect-fit clients who are so invested in making changes in their lives.

Question 5: Once you started practicing, how different or similar was reality compared to those expectations?

This step is about reckoning—with the system, the pace, the unexpected weight of the work. When reality doesn't match your expectations, it can shake your confidence or make you feel like you missed something. But often, it's not you—it's the structure you were handed. By reflecting on these early contrasts, you begin to separate your calling from the conditions. And that clarity is the first step toward realignment.

Here's a sample answer:

> Reality hit fast. I was doing more crisis management and case notes than meaningful connection. I started to feel like a mental health firefighter, constantly putting out fires, rarely able to slow down and go deep. It made me question everything. Like do I even belong here? Am I a good-enough therapist?

Question 6: Have you noticed any personal life patterns that have carried over into your professional life?

Your personal patterns don't disappear when you step into the therapist chair—they're just dressed differently. When you can name the habits that sneak into your professional life, you give yourself the power to shift them. This isn't about judgment; it's about integrity. The more you understand the echoes of your own story, the more ethically and intentionally you can show up for others.

Here's a sample answer:

> I realized I overextend myself with clients the same way I used to in relationships—saying yes when I'm exhausted, absorbing their emotions, trying to be "the fixer." It's been humbling to catch that pattern in the therapy room.

Question 7: Are there emotional or relational themes from your past that show up again and again in the clinical space?

Therapy is relational—and our history doesn't clock out when the session starts. When you notice the emotional echoes of your past in the clinical space, you're not failing your clients; you're being invited into deeper awareness. These moments offer profound opportunities to understand your countertransference, honor your boundaries, and ensure that your care is rooted in presence, not projection. Knowing your own patterns is what allows you to hold space without unconsciously filling it.

Here's a sample answer:

> Whenever I work with highly self-critical clients, I feel a pull—I want so badly to protect them from the pain I know too well. It's like I'm talking to my younger self, and I have to be mindful not to merge my story with theirs. But it's also cool to see the parallel of how clients hold different versions of myself.

Question 8: What makes your practice style unique or distinct? What have you learned through practice that school never taught you?

Your practice style is your fingerprint—it's the embodied expression of everything you've lived, learned, and unlearned. It's not about being flashy or novel; it's about being deeply *you*. When you name what makes your presence healing, you begin to trust it as valid. And when you trust it, you can articulate it. That's where clinical confidence is born—not just from mastering techniques but from understanding the impact of your way of being.

Here's a sample answer:

> Clients often say, "I feel like I can finally breathe here."
> I've learned that my calm, grounded presence does
> more than any technique ever could. School didn't
> teach me how to hold energetic space—it just taught
> interventions.

Question 9: Are there any specific modalities, practices, or processes you consistently bring into your work? What themes or interventions keep reappearing in your sessions, no matter who you're working with?

The tools you return to again and again say something about your values, your lens, and the kind of healing you believe in. When you name these patterns, you begin to see the wisdom of your own practice—not as accidental but as intuitive, intentional, and informed by lived experience. This step isn't just about listing techniques—it's about recognizing the heartbeat of your work. The through lines. The medicine. The way you show up, again and again, no matter who's sitting across from you.

Here's a sample answer:

> Many of the practices I use—like breathwork, image-
> ry, metaphor, body awareness, and spiritual reflec-
> tion—consistently show up in sessions regardless of
> the client or concern. Whether it's guiding a pause
> to regulate, asking where an emotion is felt, or ex-
> ploring meaning and intuition, these tools help cli-
> ents reconnect with their bodies and inner wisdom.
> They're not just techniques; they're part of my own
> healing journey, which is why they feel so natural and
> effective in the work.

Question 10: Out of the theories I connected with your personal story, which ones resonated and why?

It's easy to feel like your practice is "unprofessional" when it doesn't fit the conventional mold. But when a theory ech-oes back your lived experience and inner knowing, it's a game changer. It means you're not an outlier—you're part of a lineage. Naming your theoretical influences helps you reclaim your le-gitimacy and walk more boldly in your practice, not just because it "feels right" but because it's clinically and ethically grounded.

These questions aren't just busy work—they uncover what I call your clinical fingerprint: the blend of personal and pro-fessional experience that shapes how you hold space, what you prioritize in the therapy room, and what kind of transforma-tion you're built to support.

Here's a sample answer:

> When you mentioned transpersonal psychology, I felt
> emotional. It gave language to the way I've always
> worked—with reverence for intuition, symbolism, and

healing that goes beyond the mind. I didn't even know that was allowed, let alone an actual theory.

Back to Jill's Story

While reviewing Jill's professional identity reflective prompts, she wrote, "I've always sensed something deeper happening in the room—like we weren't just talking about pain, we were unraveling something sacred." That one sentence held so much truth. As I read more, I saw a pattern and connection to the transpersonal lens I had identified in her personal story.

She'd been intuitively weaving in Reiki, crystal healing, breathwork, and intuitive development for years, but she hadn't had the language to articulate why. She spoke of clients having moments of profound insight during energy sessions, of emotional releases during somatic practices on the beach, and of sensing ancestral messages during breathwork. These weren't just techniques—they were portals. And Jill knew it, even if she didn't yet have the theoretical grounding to name it.

Transpersonal psychology honors exactly this kind of work—the idea that healing isn't just psychological but also energetic, spiritual, and deeply meaningful. It invites us to see therapy as a sacred process of remembering, not just recovering. For Jill, this meant helping clients connect with their inner knowing, exploring shifts that don't always have language, and honoring the invisible forces that shape their healing. She doesn't pathologize spiritual awakening or intuitive insight. She makes room for it—because she's lived it too.

Ready to Start Exploring Your Theoretical Lens?

Now, before you get too excited—yes, I know I said in chapter 5 that I wasn't going to hand you some giant menu of theories to just pick from. And I'm still not. At least not in the way you might expect.

Here's why: I don't want you to skip the work and just start speed-reading through theories saying, *Yep, that's me, that's me, that's me!* That shortcut robs you of the actual depth this process is designed to bring.

But—let's also be real—no one else is talking about theory the way I am. So I can't just leave you hanging without a starting point.

The Top Ten Theories That Most Black Sheep Therapists Tend to Utilize

These are the ones, in my experience, that tend to resonate deeply with therapists who are drawn to integration, depth, and transformation.

If, after reading these theory snapshots, you are intrigued, I suggest you lean into learning a little bit more about each one to see if they align with your personal story of transformation and your clinical style.

1. *Psychodynamic Theory:* Psychodynamic theory, originally developed by Sigmund Freud and later expanded by figures such as Carl Jung, Melanie Klein, and Erik Erikson, focuses on understanding how unconscious processes, early life experiences, and interpersonal relationships shape an individual's behavior, emotions, and thoughts (Deal 2007). Central to this theory is the belief that much of human behavior is influenced by unconscious motives and conflicts, which are often rooted in childhood experiences.

2. *Existential-Humanistic Psychology*: Existential-humanistic psychology was developed through the combined influence of existential philosophers like Søren Kierkegaard and Martin Heidegger and humanistic psychologists such as Carl Rogers and Abraham Maslow. It emphasizes the importance of personal meaning, authentic choice, and the human capacity for growth in the face of life's uncertainties (Wertz 2023). This approach views suffering not as pathology but as a natural part of being human—offering opportunities to deepen self-awareness, purpose, and connection— while holding space for clients to confront core questions like "Who am I?" and "What truly matters?" with compassion and courage.

3. *Transpersonal Psychology*: Transpersonal psychology is a holistic approach that integrates the spiritual and transcendent aspects of the human experience into psychological understanding and practice. It goes beyond the conventional focus on the individual's mental and emotional states to explore higher states of consciousness, spiritual awakening, and the interconnectedness of all beings (Caplan, Hartelius, and Rardin 2003). Key figures include Abraham Maslow, Carl Jung, Stanislav Grof, and others.

4. *Jungian Psychology*: Jungian psychology, also known as analytical psychology, was developed by Carl Gustav Jung. It emphasizes the exploration of the unconscious mind, the integration of various aspects of the self, and the pursuit of individuation—a process of becoming one's true and whole self. Jungian psychology focuses on the interplay between the personal and collective unconscious, symbols,

and archetypes to foster psychological and spiritual growth (Gitz-Johansen 2016).

5. *Energy Psychology*: Energy psychology is a therapeutic approach that integrates principles from Eastern energy systems with Western psychological practices to address emotional and physiological distress. It operates on the premise that unresolved trauma and emotional dysregulation are not only held in the mind but also stored in the body's subtle energy fields (Feinstein and Eden 2008). It was originally pioneered by clinicians like Roger Callahan, who developed thought field therapy, and later expanded by David Feinstein and Donna Eden.

6. *Polyvagal Theory*: Polyvagal theory, developed by Dr. Stephen Porges, focuses on the role of the autonomic nervous system (ANS) in regulating emotions, social behavior, and physiological states. It provides a framework for understanding how the body's physiological responses influence emotional and relational experiences. Central to the theory is the vagus nerve, which connects the brain to various parts of the body and plays a key role in our ability to feel safe, connect with others, and respond to stress (Porges 2022).

7. *Personal Construct Theory*: Personal construct theory (PCT), developed by George Kelly, posits that individuals interpret and navigate the world through unique mental frameworks called "constructs." These constructs are personal, bipolar dimensions (e.g., success-failure, trustworthy-untrustworthy) that individuals use to make sense of their experiences, predict future events, and guide behavior (Butt and

Warren 2015). PCT emphasizes that psychological distress arises when constructs are rigid, inaccurate, or unable to accommodate new experiences.

8. *Somatic Psychology*: Somatic psychology is a holistic therapeutic approach that integrates the mind and body, emphasizing the connection between psychological processes and bodily experiences (Hartley 2004). It is rooted in the understanding that trauma, stress, and emotional experiences are not only stored in the mind but also within the body. Somatic psychology focuses on using body awareness, movement, and sensation to access and process unresolved emotional and physical trauma. Some contributors include Wilhelm Reich, Alexander Lowen, and Peter Levine.

9. *Adlerian Psychology*: Adlerian psychology, developed by Alfred Adler, focuses on the individual's drive to find purpose, belonging, and significance within their social context. It emphasizes the interconnectedness of psychological health, social interest, and lifestyle choices, suggesting that individuals strive for superiority or mastery to overcome feelings of inferiority stemming from early experiences (Ansbacher and Ansbacher 1964).

10. *Decolonization Theory*: Decolonization theory is rooted in the recognition that colonialism has left lasting impacts on individuals, communities, and societal systems. It focuses on dismantling colonial ideologies, reclaiming indigenous practices, and addressing the psychological, cultural, and systemic harm caused by colonial structures (Zapata 2020). This theory is both critical and transformative, en-

couraging individuals and communities to resist oppressive systems and reconnect with their cultural identities, histories, and wisdom.

Of course, this list is just the beginning. In my program, I offer what I call the Black Book of Conceptualized Theories—a breakdown of over thirty-three clinical theories, each mapped out with definitions, beliefs about change, case examples, references, and how they relate to both conventional and complementary practices. But for now, this list is more than enough to get you started in identifying which frameworks might mirror your journey and shape your unique practice framework.

CHAPTER 8
THE INTEGRATIVE CLINICAL PRACTICE FRAMEWORK—YOUR REBEL ROAD MAP

Now that we've explored the personal and professional story in depth, we begin channeling that insight into something more structured: the Integrative Clinical Practice Framework (ICPF). The ICPF is a cohesive blueprint that weaves together a therapist's lived experience, clinical training, theoretical alignment, and preferred modalities into one unified model of care. It's both a mirror and a map—reflecting who they are as a practitioner and guiding how they show up in the clinical space. It's a beautiful and transparent snapshot of the therapist and what can be expected for potential clients.

By this point we already have a rich foundation, but now we need to shift gears. This next phase is about helping therapists translate all that insight into clear, client-facing language that communicates their practice style with confidence and clarity.

The following are the final steps I walk clients through.

1. Write Down All the Clinical Theories That Influence Your Practice

Sometimes the first draft of your framework can feel like messy artwork—it's colorful, layered, and meaningful, but it's not yet refined. This step is about cleaning it up.

Often, we think one theory is *the* foundation, only to realize later that it's actually encompassed by another or that it's not as central as we first thought. For example, both transpersonal psychology and Jungian psychology emphasize the importance of the unconscious and spirituality, but they differ in scope—one leans more into archetypes and symbols, while the other frames healing as a spiritual journey of wholeness. You may find that both fit or that one captures your essence more fully. This is the moment of confirmation and clarity.

Shifting to a clean worksheet or a fresh sheet of paper helps, because the earlier prompts often carry raw emotion. Now we're stepping into structure.

As a reminder, while the example of Jill I just reviewed only focused on one theory for simplicity, most of the therapists I work with draw from five to ten different theoretical influences. You don't have to box yourself into one. This is about building something that reflects *you*—your story, your practice, your unique blend of clinical insight and lived experience.

Here are some examples:

Attachment theory
Transpersonal psychology
Polyvagal theory
Humanistic theory
Energy psychology
Psychodynamic theory

2. Reflect and Speak on Why These Theories Matter to You

This step is about connection, not overthinking. If you find yourself stumbling or second-guessing why a theory belongs, pause and ask, Is *this really mine*? Theories that truly fit your story should feel like old friends—you don't have to dig too deep to explain why they matter.

I invite you to make this reflection personal. These aren't just abstract frameworks; they're mirrors of your values, beliefs about healing, and the way you already work with clients every day.

This reflection should come quickly—if a theory really shapes the way you practice, you'll feel it in your bones. Think about how it shows up in the therapy room.

Here's a sample answer:

- *Polyvagal Theory*: "This keeps me attuned to nervous system shifts. I track breath, tone, and posture so I know when to slow down, pause, or help clients ground before we move deeper."
- *Psychodynamic Theory*: "This shapes the way I listen. I'm always noticing themes, patterns, and unconscious slips that point to what's unspoken in the room."
- *Humanistic Theory*: "My practice is built around authenticity. I focus less on technique and more on being fully present, meeting clients with unconditional positive regard."
- *Attachment Theory*: "This guides how I structure safety in the relationship. I pay close attention to ruptures and repairs and how clients experience me as a secure base."

3. Communicate This to Clients in a Way They Can Understand

It's one thing to know what theories influence you—it's another to translate that into language clients can hear and trust. This step is about shifting from clinical jargon to plain, human words. Think of it as your *client-facing translation*.

The question here is, What do you want your clients to understand about how you work? What's the tone, message, or reassurance you want them to feel when they sit across from you?

Here's a sample answer:

- *Polyvagal Theory*: "I want clients to know that their bodies aren't betraying them—they're protecting them. I'll say something like, 'Your nervous system has been working overtime to keep you safe. Together, we'll help it learn new ways to feel steady and supported.'"

- *Psychodynamic Theory*: "I want clients to understand that their patterns make sense. I might explain it as, 'Sometimes the past sneaks into the present without us realizing it. Our work will help you notice these patterns so they don't keep running the show.'"

- *Attachment Theory*: "I want clients to know therapy is a safe relationship where healing can happen. I'll say, 'Even if safety has felt shaky in other parts of your life, we'll practice building it here together.'"

- *Transpersonal Psychology*: "I want clients to feel free to explore meaning and spirituality if it matters to them. I might put it this way: 'Sometimes healing isn't just about managing symptoms—it's about rediscovering purpose, connection, or even a sense of the sacred.'"

If someone gets stuck here, a guiding prompt could be, "If a brand-new client asked you what working with you feels like, how would you explain it without using theory words?"

The goal is to move beyond theory and into voice. It's about distilling your framework into something your clients can actually feel when you speak it. Theories give you the scaffolding, but your language gives it life.

And we want it to carry your voice, your humor, your heart. If you're someone who curses in session? Say that. If you crack jokes, quote poetry, or have a signature tagline that clients remember long after session—bring it in. Write until it feels like a snapshot of what it's like to sit with you.

I feel like examples help, so I am including my ICPF to help you get a better idea of what I mean.

My Integrative Clinical Practice Framework

My practice—and the complementary and alternative interventions I integrate—are informed by an unapologetically integrative theoretical framework grounded in existential-humanistic theory, psychodynamic theory, Jungian psychology, and transpersonal psychology.

I'm not your "typical therapist." I will never bring something into the room that I haven't personally lived, questioned, wrestled with, or tried myself. That's not just a preference; it's a promise. I believe that modeling the work is part of the work. And I hold the privilege of this space with deep reverence.

This means I approach healing as both a sacred and psychological process. I hold space for the questions that don't have easy answers—Who am I? What's my purpose? Why is this happening? When will this stop happening?—and I trust that meaning is born in the mess, not the perfection. Healing doesn't come from tidying things up or rushing to solutions. It comes from staying and sitting with compassion, with presence, with the hard stuff. Because shame doesn't create change, safety does. [existential-humanistic]

I believe that the past lives in the present. Unconscious beliefs, protective strategies, ancestral wounds, and early attachment patterns don't just vanish with insight; they echo through our relationships, our bodies, and our ways of staying "safe." I help you explore those patterns with curiosity instead of criticism without needing to fix, label, or exile them. [psychodynamic theory]

I believe that there is a part of you that is intuitive, sacred, and wildly wise, even if it's been buried under a survival mode. My work is about helping that part of you reawaken. Whether that's through soul purpose, spiritual exploration, or the quiet remembering of your inner truth—this work isn't about fixing you. It's about helping you reclaim who you've always been and making space for who you're still becoming. [transpersonal and Jungian psychology]

And if I'm being honest, I joke a lot that healing is kind of a scam. Not because it's fake but because the idea that one day you'll "arrive" fully healed and never get triggered again? Yeahhhh, okay. If you are lucky, healing is ongoing. It's layered. Cyclical. And it's often uncomfortable. And at the same time, it's transformative, expansive, and even a little fun.

Most importantly, this is your healing, not mine. I don't position myself above you. I sit beside you. I believe you've adapted with brilliance to systems, stories, and cycles that were never designed to support your full self. Together, we'll walk toward a version of transformation that doesn't just soothe your pain but expands your possibilities.

That right there—that's my theoretical framework. But more than that, it's the heartbeat of my practice. It's my real, raw belief system about what I do, why I do it, and what clients can expect when they work with me.

When someone reads this, they get a crystal-clear sense of the energy I bring, the kind of space I hold, and the way I walk beside them in the healing process. It's meant to spark a reaction—either "Hell yes, I want to work with her," or "Nope, not my vibe." And honestly? That's exactly the point.

Do clients care about theoretical frameworks? Maybe not in the academic sense. What they care about is whether you will understand them. Whether you can help them. Whether the way you work actually *works*.

But let's be real—the process of choosing a therapist is often overwhelming and disheartening. Clients scroll through *Psychology Today* profiles or websites filled with the same polished, generic language—and walk away with no real sense of who they're about to open up to.

Most of us weren't trained in marketing, niching, or how to articulate the depth of what we do. That's why this process matters.

It gives you clarity, confidence, and language that reflects your essence—not just your education. It blends your personality, your clinical lens, your beliefs, and your lived experience into something clients can feel. And when clients can *feel* your work before they ever meet you? That's self-determination in action. It empowers them to choose with discernment, not desperation.

How You Can Work on Your Own Framework

Now, this didn't come to me overnight. I've rewritten and refined this statement several times over the years, and that's normal. Your language will evolve as you do. The more confident I became in my style and in the power of what I bring, the more fluidly I could speak on it. What you see now is the result of that growth—but it still sounds like *me*. It reflects my personality. It's grounded in both clinical theory *and* spiritual insight. It doesn't play small. That's what I want for you too.

If you're doing this on your own, feel free to use my example for inspiration—but don't let it define you. Some therapists I work with write just a few powerful lines. Others create something more expansive.

There's no right length, no perfect structure. This is about what feels aligned with your truth.

Should you choose to share this information on your website, you have the option to remove the theory at the end of the sentence. That part is just for us, so you can see how your deepest truths and beliefs are, in fact, grounded in a clinical lens. It's proof that your magic and your methods aren't just floating around unanchored—they have a solid foundation. However, I do leave the theories in the statement for my informed consent, but I will get to that soon.

Again, this is the first step in identifying your clinical identity. It's what sets the stage for integrating those complementary, spiritual, or energy-based modalities you've wanted to bridge into your work in an ethical, powerful, and aligned way.

CHAPTER 9
THE CLINICAL FUSION BLUEPRINT—FROM CHAOS TO CLARITY (PART 1)

The Clinical Fusion Blueprint is where your integration work becomes concrete. Up until now, we've talked about theory, ethics, scope, and competency—but this is where you start putting the pieces together into something tangible.

Think of it as your practice's "translation guide." It's the clear, transparent explanation of exactly what you're bringing into the therapy room—whether that's Reiki, crystal healing, aromatherapy, tarot, sound therapy, or any other complementary or alternative intervention.

This isn't just a poetic description; it's a detailed, client-facing explanation that sets expectations, removes guesswork, and eliminates the "mystery" that can get therapists in trouble with boards, lawyers, or clients.

In the Clinical Fusion Blueprint process, you will

- *Name and describe the practice*—in plain, accessible language your clients can understand, without jargon or assumptions. You will also highlight the potential benefits that they can experience from the integration.

- *Identify the risks and disclaimers*—Every intervention has them, and clients deserve to know them up front.
- *Align the practice with your clinical framework*—weaving in the theoretical lens that justifies its use in your role as a licensed mental health professional.
- *Reference research*—showing that your choice to use it is grounded in something more than intuition alone.

Before we talk about theory or research, we start with the *how* and the *what*. What does this practice look like in your space? How does it work? Is it hands-on, hands-off, or entirely verbal? Is it in person, virtual, or both? Does it involve scents, sounds, movement, or touch? Where will you be positioned in relation to the client? What choices will they have to tailor it to their comfort level?

This is your opportunity to add your personal touch—to capture not just what the modality is in general but what it looks like when *you* facilitate it. When done well, this section is more than just a description. It's an invitation for clients to make an informed choice about their participation and a clear record you can stand behind ethically and professionally.

Name the Practice

The starting point is simple: Name the modality exactly as you would in your informed consent or professional documentation. Avoid vague titles like "energy work" unless you're pairing them with a specific name (e.g., "Reiki energy healing").

Things to keep in mind:

- State the exact name of the practice (e.g., "Reiki," "Oracle Cards," "Aromatherapy").
- If it has a recognized lineage, system, or tradition, include it (e.g., "Usui Reiki" rather than just "Reiki").
- If your practice blends multiple approaches, be explicit (e.g., "Intuitive tarot readings combined with guided imagery").
- Use the practice name consistently across your paperwork, website, and marketing materials to avoid confusion (e.g., Reiki energy healing vs. energy practice).

Let me add an important note regarding language and trademarks. Be careful not to use terms just because they "sound professional." Some modalities are trademarked or proprietary systems created by specific individuals or organizations. For example, Psychotherapeutic Reiki is a formal, trademarked method, with its own trainings and certification process. Simply using Reiki in psychotherapy does not mean you can call your work Psychotherapeutic Reiki. To avoid liability or misrepresentation, only use these protected names if you have received the proper training and certification.

Description of the Practice

This is the client-friendly overview—clear enough for someone with zero prior knowledge to understand what it is and grounded enough that it could be read by a state board reviewer without raising red flags.

Things to keep in mind:

- Use plain, accessible language—avoid unexplained jargon.

- Include origin or lineage only if relevant to cultural accuracy or ethical transparency.
- State its general purpose and how it supports therapeutic goals.
- Keep it objective—focus on what the practice *involves* and potential benefits, rather than making unverifiable claims.

What It Looks Like in Your Practice (Personalization)

This is where you paint the picture—giving clients a step-by-step visual of what happens in the room, so they feel safe, informed, and clear on their consent.

Things to keep in mind:

- *Location:* Is it in your therapy office, outdoors, or virtual?
- *Client Position:* Sitting, lying down, moving?
- *Practitioner Position:* Where are you in relation to the client?
- *Tools:* Are there objects (cards, crystals, oils, bowls) used?
- *Sensory Elements:* Lighting, music, scents, temperature?
- *Client Role:* Are they passive (receiving) or active (engaging in dialogue, movement, visualization)?
- *Boundaries:* Is touch involved? If so, where and how is consent obtained?
- *Structure:* How long does this segment last, and is it woven into the therapy session or stand-alone?

Let's look at some examples.

Usui Shiki Ryoho Reiki

Name of the Practice:
Usui Shiki Ryoho Reiki

Description of the Practice:
Usui Reiki is a Japanese healing practice developed in the early twentieth century within the Usui lineage. It is designed to promote relaxation, reduce stress, and support emotional well-being by creating a safe and calm environment in which the body's natural capacity for balance can emerge. In clinical practice, Reiki is not framed as a cure or a replacement for medical care but as a complementary method that can help prepare the nervous system for therapeutic work, such as trauma processing and integration.

Personalized Application in Practice:
In session, clients remain fully clothed and may lie comfortably on a massage-style table or sit upright in a chair, depending on their preference and accessibility needs. The practitioner places hands either gently on, near, or above specific areas of the body—such as the head, shoulders, torso, or knees—holding each position for several minutes. There is no manipulation of muscles or joints. The session environment often includes soft music or nature sounds, dim lighting, and blankets for comfort. Sessions last anywhere from ten to thirty minutes within a therapy appointment, depending on therapeutic goals. Clients often report a sense of deep calm, emotional release, and improved grounding after Reiki. Clear consent is always obtained before touch is used, and clients may choose a hands-off approach at any time.

Aromatherapy

Name of the Practice:
Aromatherapy

Description of the Practice:
Aromatherapy involves the therapeutic use of essential oils derived from aromatic plants. Its history spans thousands of years, with modern practice focusing on emotional and psychological support through scent. Within therapy, aromatherapy is not a stand-alone treatment but a tool to enhance relaxation, regulation, and grounding, helping clients anchor themselves in the present moment during or after emotionally intense work.

Personalized Application in Practice:
Aromatherapy is offered in session through safe, bounded methods of inhalation. Clients may hold an inhaler stick near the nose, breathe from a drop of oil on a tissue, or experience a gentle room diffusion. If topical application is offered, oils are diluted in a carrier and applied only with explicit consent, typically to the wrists or temples. Direct ingestion of essential oils is never encouraged. Scents may be chosen collaboratively—for example, lavender for calming, citrus for uplifting, or peppermint for alertness. The sensory element of smell helps many clients regulate their emotional state, recall memories, or transition from trauma processing into closure.

Oracle/Tarot Cards

Name of the Practice:
Oracle and Tarot Cards

Description of the Practice:
　　Oracle and tarot cards are symbolic tools historically used for storytelling, reflection, and insight. Tarot originated in fifteenth-century Europe as playing cards, later developing into a system rich with archetypal and metaphorical imagery. Oracle decks, often more contemporary, vary in theme and design. In a therapeutic context, these cards are not used for fortune-telling but as a way to invite curiosity, surface subconscious material, and create metaphor-rich dialogue that supports the client's process.

Personalized Application in Practice:
　　During a session, the therapist and client sit together at a table or in chairs. A deck is selected collaboratively—either from the therapist's collection or brought by the client. The client is invited to shuffle and draw cards themselves or may ask the therapist to do so. Once cards are laid out, the imagery becomes a conversational starting point: Clients reflect on what symbols, colors, or scenes evoke for them. The environment is typically quiet to allow focus, sometimes with soft background music if helpful. Card work is integrated into therapy rather than standing apart, often serving as a bridge to deeper dialogue, metaphor exploration, or parts work. The practice is client-led, with emphasis on empowerment and personal meaning rather than prescriptive interpretations.

Risks and Disclaimers

As with any therapeutic approach, it's essential to provide clear, transparent information about the scope, limitations, and potential risks of these practices. While modalities such as Reiki, aromatherapy, and the use of oracle or tarot cards can offer meaningful support for relaxation, grounding, and self-reflection, they are not without important considerations. Since they are being integrated alongside psychotherapy, each practice carries its own boundaries, safety guidelines, and ethical responsibilities. By outlining these risks and disclaimers, we create a shared understanding between client and clinician—one that protects both parties, ensures informed choice, and upholds the integrity of the therapeutic process.

Usui Shiki Ryoho Reiki

- Reiki is not a substitute for medical, psychiatric, or emergency care. It does not involve diagnosing conditions, prescribing treatments, or manipulating the body.
- Some clients may experience temporary emotional release (e.g., tearfulness, fatigue, or heightened sensitivity) as part of the relaxation process. These experiences typically pass within twenty-four to forty-eight hours.
- Reiki involves light, near, or no touch, always over clothing. Clients are encouraged to voice any discomfort with hand placement or session pacing. Touch is never applied to sensitive or inappropriate areas.

Aromatherapy/Essential Oils

- Essential oils are for external use and inhalation only in this setting. They are never ingested or swallowed, as this may cause harm.
- Oils used on the skin are diluted in a carrier oil and applied only with informed consent. Clients should immediately notify the therapist of any allergies, asthma, pregnancy, or skin sensitivities before use.
- Possible risks include allergic reactions, headaches, nausea, or respiratory irritation, particularly if sensitivity is unknown. Oils will always be introduced slowly and discontinued if discomfort arises.

Oracle/Tarot Cards

- Oracle and tarot cards are used as a therapeutic tool for reflection and meaning making, not for fortune-telling or predicting future events.
- Clients maintain full autonomy in how they interpret the imagery and are invited to decline or redirect the process at any time.
- Some imagery may evoke strong emotions or memories. This is part of the therapeutic dialogue and will be processed safely within the session.

Why a Touch Disclaimer Matters

Another myth that comes up all the time: "You can't use touch in therapy."

Insert game show buzzer sound here. Wrong. Totally wrong.

Now, if you've been with me throughout this book, you already know the next line. Ready? Say it with me: It depends.

It depends on how your state board and your professional code of ethics define and regulate touch in practice. And you know what's next: It's vague! Which leaves you where? Yep—open to interpretation.

So, what do you do when it's open to interpretation? You prove your understanding of the interpretation. With clear documentation. With informed consent. With theory alignment. What have they won, Scotty? More paperwork!

Any time touch is introduced into a therapeutic setting—whether through Reiki, aromatherapy application, or simple grounding gestures like a hand on the shoulder—it must be framed with legal, ethical, and client-safety boundaries. This isn't just about liability. It's about transparency, consent, and protecting both you and your client from misunderstandings.

And something I would like to additionally mention: Therapeutic Touch (TT) is a trademarked and formalized energy-based nursing modality developed in the 1970s by Dolores Krieger, PhD and Dora Kunz. Simply incorporating touch into therapy does not mean you are practicing Therapeutic Touch. You cannot use that label unless you are trained and certified in TT.

Examples from State Laws and Codes of Ethics Regarding Touch

Texas: The Texas Behavioral Health Executive Council (2023) does not mention specific language around touch in therapy. There are rules around setting and maintaining professional boundaries, but they don't specifically authorize nonsexual touch. The rules require you to take reasonable precautions to protect clients from physical or emotional harm.

California: Similarly, the California Board of Behavioral Sciences (2023) does not explicitly mention touch; however, it emphasizes protecting client safety, avoiding harmful conduct, and maintaining professional boundaries.

New York: The New York State Office of the Professions (n.d.) provides guidance in their article entitled "Maintaining Appropriate Professional Boundaries," which explicitly advises that clinicians should avoid hugging or other physical contact that blurs professional boundaries, and if such contact seems appropriate, you should seek the client's consent to reduce risk of misinterpretation.

Florida: The Board of Clinical Social Work, Marriage and Family Therapy, and Mental Health Counseling (2023) has no accessible, explicit language in the current statutes or administrative rules about touch in psychotherapy for these license types. Their statutes do highlight that any sexualized or exploitative physical contact is explicitly prohibited, and all clinician actions must align with professional competency and avoid exploitation.

Maryland: Okay, I have to be honest with you. Midway through writing this book, I had completely lost hope that a single state would say anything—anything!—remotely useful about touch in therapy. I was knee-deep in vague language, boundary buzzwords, and a whole lot of "interpret at your own risk."

And then . . . bam!

Here comes Maryland, strutting in like the overachiever in a group project, with actual regulations. You didn't just show up, you showed out. Maryland's Board of Professional Counselors and Therapists' ethics code (2023) says,

> A counselor engaging in nontraditional treatment modalities [okay, Maryland, I see you] using physical contact with a client shall document in the client record:

1) An assessment of the client;
2) A written rationale for the use of the physical contact treatment modality;
3) A copy of the informed consent signed and dated by both the client and the counselor, which addresses:
    a) The risks and benefits of the physical contact;
    b) The objectives and intended outcomes;
    c) Available alternative interventions; and
    d) A description of the physical contact that may be reasonably anticipated.
4) Furthermore, a counselor may not engage in physical contact if the risk of psychological harm outweighs the potential benefits, even if the client requests it.

Honestly? Respect.

Maryland got this one right—clear, structured, client-centered. It's not anti-touch. It's pro informed, intentional, and clear engagement around the use of touch.

Now, if the rest of the country could just take notes . . .

The key is this: If your state is vague (which I am guessing it is), you need to ground your rationale in theory, client consent, documentation, and probably take a cue from Maryland's outline.

That means—describe the type of touch you use, name the potential benefits, identify the risks and disclaimers, explain how it aligns with clinical theory, and reference research that supports its integration in psychotherapy.

In other words, don't reinvent the wheel. Follow the same framework. Because when you document touch this way, you're not only protecting yourself ethically—you're also giving your clients the clarity and safety they deserve.

Additional Disclaimer: Touch and Massage Therapy

As we have reviewed, every state (and every licensing board) has its own language around what's permissible. Massage therapy, in particular, is a separately regulated profession in most states, requiring its own license. That means a clinician who is *also* a licensed massage therapist may have a wider scope than one who is only licensed as a counselor or social worker.

I am bringing this up because there is a strong consensus that the state of Florida requires you to have a massage therapy license to practice Reiki for compensation. There is no law that actually states this, but previous legal rulings and blogs strongly suggest that this may be the case. Now, before you have an internal panic, this is very different from what we have been discussing because we are engaging in integrative work—offering psychotherapy while integrating complementary therapies within a theoretical framework. But if it can possibly impact you and your practice, you need to become educated around it.

Failing to check the rules is more than a paperwork issue—it's a liability. Engaging in physical touch without knowing your state's stance can expose you to complaints for "boundary violations" or "unprofessional conduct." Even if your intent is therapeutic, regulators look at consent, clarity, and scope. If a client files a complaint, your defense rests not on your intent but on whether your action was *permitted* and *documented* within your license.

For this reason, I encourage therapists to make "regulatory follow-up" a standard step in their integration process. Here's what this follow-up should entail:

- *Check your licensing board.* Review your profession's official rules (not just hearsay from colleagues). Look specifically for sections on scope of practice, boundaries, and prohibited conduct. Educate yourself on additional licensing bodies that regulate the modalities you are additionally trained in.
- *Differentiate licenses.* If you hold multiple licenses (e.g., massage therapy and counseling), clarify when you are practicing under which license, and make sure your informed consent spells that out.
- *Err on the side of clarity.* When in doubt, assume touch is a high-risk area that requires extra layers of consent, documentation, and transparency.
- *Revisit regularly.* Regulations evolve. A board may issue updated guidance, policy statements, or even disciplinary cases that set new precedents. Make it part of your professional ethics to review your state rules at least once a year.

In other words, before you integrate touch or body-based interventions, know exactly where your license stands. This is part of being both an ethical and empowered practitioner. You don't need to scare clients with legal language, but you do need to ground yourself in your state's expectations so your work is as safe as it is transformative.

Okay, are you still with me? Let's shift to part two of the Clinical Fusion Blueprint: alignment and research.

Chapter 10
The Clinical Fusion Blueprint— From Chaos to Clarity (Part 2)

Up to this point, you've mapped your practice framework— the set of theories that reflect how you believe healing happens. Now it's time to take the next step: weaving those theories into the modalities you practice.

This is where we move from *parallel tracks* (theory on one side, modalities on the other) into fusion language—the bridge that shows exactly how your clinical framework and chosen practices align.

1. Gather Your Ingredients

Take out the lists you created in earlier chapters:

- Your identified theories (these are your anchor points)
- Your modalities (the CAIs, somatic tools, or spiritual practices you're trained in)
- Your notes on why each theory matters to you (found in the "From Magic to Method" worksheet)

Having these side by side keeps the connections visible and accessible.

2. Establish Your Rule of Alignment

Here's the nonnegotiable guideline:

- Every modality you integrate should be aligned with at least two to three theoretical frameworks from your ICPF.
- Every theory you listed in your practice framework must appear under at least one modality.

Why? Because this ensures your practice is balanced—no theory is just "window dressing," and no modality is floating without a solid clinical backbone.

3. Start the Pairing Process

Now look at your list and begin creating fusion statements. Complete the following steps for each modality:

1. Write, in your own words, a brief description of the process and benefits.
2. Then, match it with the theory (or theories) that naturally connect to that theme. For example, Reiki aligns with energy psychology (biofield awareness), attachment theory (therapeutic attunement), and transpersonal psychology (connection to something larger than self).
3. Put them side by side: modality description plus theoretical alignment.

Don't worry—I'll walk you through an example in just a minute.

4. Notice Themes

As you write, patterns will emerge. Maybe you tend to see everything through an attachment lens—that's fine. Or maybe you notice that somatic theories show up again and again when you describe your work—also fine. These themes become the *signature* of your practice.

5. Keep It Transparent

This exercise isn't just for paperwork—it's for clarity. When you can clearly say, "Here's how Reiki aligns with my professional training, and my framework is rooted in somatic psychology and transpersonal theory," you're not only protecting yourself ethically; you're building trust with your clients and confidence in your practice.

On page 125 is an example of what I want you to start building for yourself. I highly suggest you review this chart before moving on.

Breaking everything down and seeing the themes and alignment will help you build the language that you will transfer into your informed consent. We are going to use this table to help you ground your practice within a theoretical frame—building something tangible to justify the integrative practice. Let's look at some examples below.

Reiki and Energy Psychology

From an energy psychology perspective, Reiki supports therapeutic work by helping clients shift energetic imbalances that may underlie emotional distress. The integration of Reiki into psychotherapy allows clients to experience both cognitive insight and somatic release, enhancing the body-mind con-

Alignment Table

1. Reiki
Brief description:
A gentle energy practice where the therapist uses light touch or hands hovering near the body to support emotional regulation, release energetic blocks, and promote balance.

Theoretical Alignment:
Energy Psychology: Emphasizes biofield awareness and shifting stuck patterns.
Attachment Theory: Provides safety and co-regulation with therapeutic attunement.
Transpersonal Psychology: Opens connection to a sense of the sacred or higher self.

Shared Themes:
Restoring flow and safety—helping clients feel both energetically balanced and relationally supported.

2. Tarot/Oracle Cards
Brief description:
Symbolic cards are used to spark reflection, surface unconscious material, and open dialogue about meaning, identity, and choice.

Theoretical Alignment:
Psychodynamic Theory: Externalizes unconscious material and projections.
Existential-Humanistic Theory: Encourages self-reflection, choice, and meaning-making.
Transpersonal Psychology: Provides a bridge to archetypal and spiritual insight.

Shared Themes:
Bringing the unseen into awareness—making hidden stories and inner truths visible in a safe, reflective process.

3. Crystals
Brief description:
Crystals are used for symbolic resonance and grounding, offering clients a tangible anchor during emotional processing or ritual.

Theoretical Alignment:
Somatic Psychology: Provides sensory grounding and nervous system regulation.
Jungian/Archetypal Psychology: Emphasizes how crystals embody symbolic/archetypal meaning.
Ecopsychology: Honors the healing role of nature and natural elements.

Shared Themes:
Anchoring presence—creating tangible, symbolic connections that ground clients in both body and meaning.

nection and supporting resilience. This supports energy psychology by grounding the therapeutic process in the understanding that emotional healing can occur through shifts in the body's energetic systems.

Tarot/Oracle Cards and Transpersonal Psychology

From a transpersonal psychology perspective, tarot or oracle cards serve as symbolic tools that invite clients to access deeper layers of meaning, spirituality, or personal transformation. The integration of these cards into therapy creates opportunities for clients to explore archetypal themes, cultivate insight, and reconnect with a sense of purpose or sacredness in their healing process. This supports transpersonal psychology by validating the role of spiritual exploration and symbolic meaning in promoting psychological growth and transformation.

Crystals and Somatic Psychology

From a somatic psychology perspective, crystals function as grounding tools that engage sensory awareness and support nervous system regulation. The integration of crystals into therapy helps clients anchor themselves in the present moment, deepen embodiment, and maintain stability while working through emotionally charged material. This supports somatic psychology by emphasizing the importance of body-based practices that strengthen regulation, embodiment, and the integration of mind and body in the healing process.

Making the Missing Link Visible

In chapter 2, we reviewed myths about ethical practices. Then we took a deeper dive into how regulatory bodies defined scope of practice and defined practiced applications. Remember the vague language they used, such as "interventions grounded in theory" and "utilize principles of counseling and social work into practice."

These statements basically are telling us that we should avoid using modalities that can't be theoretically justified. But because literally no one (except me) teaches you how to do that, building that language and alignment can feel abstract or intimidating. This leaves many therapists unsure of how to bridge their genuine interest in complementary practices with their professional obligations.

By mapping complementary and alternative interventions—such as Reiki, tarot cards, or crystals—onto established psychological theories, we make the implicit explicit. What once sounded like vague academic directives becomes concrete, usable clinical language.

This approach provides you with a *theoretical backbone* for your integrative work: a way to demonstrate that your chosen practices not only make sense in a therapeutic context but also support and enhance the clinical goals.

This process does more than satisfy compliance requirements. *It empowers therapists.*

Instead of fearing that your creativity or intuition has no place in therapy, you can now document with confidence, articulate your rationale with clarity, and affirm to clients, colleagues, or licensing boards: "Here is the theoretical justification for this practice. Here is why it belongs in therapy."

Mic drop!

Research

In earlier chapters, we explored the importance of grounding your work in evidence-based frameworks, which includes staying current with the best available research on the modalities and interventions you bring into your clinical practice. This doesn't just mean keeping up with trends—it means engaging with published research like meta-analyses, systematic reviews, case studies, and qualitative findings as part of responsible integration.

One of the most common things I hear from therapists after taking training in a new modality is this: "The developer has been doing a ton of research on this for years." And my immediate question is always, "Great—but is it published? Is it available for review?"

And yet—here's what I often find: a beautifully designed website, a packed certification program, glowing testimonials, maybe even a "research" tab . . . and then? Just a list of other people's studies loosely related to the topic, but not a single published study on the actual modality being taught. I'll never understand it.

You mean to tell me you have over five thousand people certified in this approach and not one peer-reviewed article to show for it? If I had a modality with that kind of reach, you better believe I'd be conducting research—or hiring someone who could. Give your work a backbone. Give it something people can build on. Something future clinicians can cite, challenge, replicate, and evolve. Otherwise, what are we even doing?

But then there are the few who are doing the research—which is amazing. The problem? They keep it in-house. The real impact only happens when that research is published, peer-reviewed, and accessible—not just mentioned in a training slide or tossed into a webinar. That's what allows the broader field to evaluate it, replicate it, and take it seriously.

And look, I get it. Research and publication aren't easy. A 2015 study suggests there can be a seventeen-year lag between when health-related research is conducted and when it's fully translated into practice (Hanney et al. 2015). That timeline includes everything—data collection, analysis, writing, peer review, and final publication.

Personally, I remember being so wiped after graduation that I wasn't sure I'd ever revisit my dissertation. But I did. I trimmed it down, got support, and submitted it—because I didn't want to contribute to the silence. Today, it's published under the title "Licensed Clinical Social Workers' Perceptions of Complementary and Alternative Interventions," coauthored with Dr. Morgan Cooley and Dr. Darren Weissman.

Here's the reality: Many modalities may claim a research base, but unless that research has actually made it through peer review and into journals, we can't rely on it as "evidence."

It's not about doubting innovation—it's about accountability and transparency. If we want to integrate complementary practices or emerging practices responsibly, it's our job to check what actually exists, rather than just repeating what we've been told.

And part of professionalism is not only doing this homework for ourselves but also making that research available to our clients. Even if they never ask for it, the very fact that you can point them to studies demonstrates integrity, transparency, and an ethic of informed choice.

The Frustrating Gatekeeping of Research

Now let's talk about how messy this process really is. The first thing you'll encounter when you start searching is not peer-reviewed articles but a flood of blogs, summaries, or popular media sites like *Psychology Today*. Interesting? Maybe. Evidence? No.

When you finally do find what you're looking for—an actual journal article—you'll often hit another wall: a forty-to-six-ty-dollar paywall just to download it. It's wild but true. I still remember the moment my own dissertation was published and I realized I couldn't even access it for free. I even emailed the journal directly for a copy and never heard back. I had to rely on a colleague affiliated with a university to download it for me. Imagine: my own research, locked behind a paywall. That is the definition of systemic gatekeeping.

And this is where a lot of therapists get stuck—they wonder, *Is it really my obligation to dig through this?* In an ideal world, no. Research that informs clinical practice should be openly available. But the truth is, right now it isn't. So if we want to stay ahead, we need strategies.

Where to Start Looking

- *Google Scholar*: Always my first stop. Use the filters on the left to limit to *research articles* instead of just books or commentary. Play around with different keyword combinations to cast a wide net.
- *Copy and paste titles*: If you find an article on Google Scholar but can't access it, copy the title and drop it into a regular Google search. You'd be surprised how often you'll uncover a free PDF floating around— sometimes even uploaded by the author themselves. Sometimes you can request an article from an author; however, I have done this a hundred times and never received a response.

- *Think beyond mental health*: Don't just stick to psychology journals. Look in adjacent fields like nursing, medicine, integrative health, transpersonal psychology, or energy medicine. A lot of complementary practices are studied outside the strict mental health silo.
- *Build your own resource list*: When I find a relevant article, I like to save the link and sometimes even include it directly in my informed consent documents for that modality. You can also just add a proper reference so clients can follow up themselves. It's a small act of transparency that says, "Here's what exists—take a look if you'd like."

Doing this work isn't about proving a point—it's about practicing with integrity. By knowing what research exists, naming what doesn't, and being transparent about both, we build trust with our clients and credibility for our field. Yes, the system of research publication is flawed. Yes, it's exhausting. But every time we bridge the gap, we chip away at that larger failure and make the work just a little more accessible.

Evaluating the Research You Find

Once you find the research, your job isn't over—you now have an extra layer of professional responsibility. You have to assess the strength and limitations of the evidence. Not all research is generalizable, and not all findings carry clinical significance.

A single case study doesn't make a modality *empirically supported*, but it can make it evidence-informed—and that matters. Qualitative and case-based work often provides the early data that helps a new modality grow its foundation.

At the same time, we can't treat every new study like it's gold. Our job is to ask,

Who was studied?

What were the outcome measures?

Does this apply to my clients?

What might be missing from the data?

Clinical relevance and statistical significance are not the same thing. For many emerging, spiritual, or somatic modalities, research may be in its early stages, but that doesn't mean it lacks value. It just means we hold it with curiosity, not certainty.

The Critique of Empirically Supported Treatments (ESTs)

And while we're here, let's talk about the so-called "gold standard": empirically supported treatments (ESTs), widely referenced by the Facebook keyboard warriors—please know they're not without critique.

Researchers have long pointed out that many ESTs are built on narrow participant samples, often privileging white, Western, middle-class populations and overlooking cultural, relational, and spiritual dimensions of healing (Sue et al. 2009).

Others question the over-reliance on randomized controlled trials (RCTs) as the only acceptable form of evidence, noting that this approach strips away the nuance of real-world clinical practice and the therapeutic relationship (Castelnuovo 2004).

Meta-reviews have also revealed that the evidential strength of many so-called "empirically supported" psychotherapies is far weaker than often claimed (Sakaluk et al. 2019). Even when effective, ESTs often lose potency in community or diverse cultural settings (Schneider 2020).

As Lilienfeld (2013) points out, many clinicians resist the EST model not because they're anti-science but because they see how rigid adherence to it can erase client individuality, cultural complexity, and therapist intuition.

So yes—evidence matters. But so does context. So does lived experience. So does the art of therapy.

A healthy field doesn't worship the data—it converses with it.

CHAPTER 11
BRINGING IT ALL TOGETHER—FROM FRAMEWORK TO FREEDOM

So here we are. You've reflected on your personal journey. You've aligned with theories that speak to your truth. You've explored the clinical language that honors your intuitive gifts, your energetic lens, your spiritual integrity. You've done the soul work and the scope-of-practice work. And now?

Now we bring it all together.

Now we make it legit.

Now we write it into the very heartbeat of your practice: your informed consent.

As we previously spoke about, your informed consent isn't just a form. It's your first act of transparency. It's your first clinical intervention. It's a legal document, yes, but it's also a declaration of who you are, how you work, what clients can expect, and what you've done to make sure you're showing up with both competence and care.

It shouldn't be a form that only covers fees, cancellations, confidentiality, and maybe a sentence or two about therapy goals. That's not enough.

Not when you are an innovator.

Not when you're integrating energy-based, spiritual, complementary, or other emerging interventions.

Not when you're a trailblazer who colors outside the clinical lines.

Not when your entire practice style is built on an intentional fusion of theory and transformation.

So let's reframe this.

Your informed consent isn't just a form. It's a clinical anchor, a legal mirror of your competence, and a declaration of transparency that protects both you and your clients.

Education and Training

The first thing I tell every clinician in my program is this: If you're going to integrate any modality into your psychotherapy practice, you need to prove that you're competent to use it. This isn't a philosophical statement—this is legal, ethical, and required in most professional codes and state board regulations.

And don't get lazy here. I don't want to see "I'm trained in energy work." I want to see training hours, instructor names, lineages, and credentialing bodies when applicable. This isn't about gatekeeping your magic. This is about backing up your magic with professional clarity. Competency is not optional—and as I've said throughout this book, you must be able to justify your integration to the depth that you're offering it.

Here's what I include (and what I recommend every therapist spell out):

- Your full professional title (e.g., Licensed Clinical Social Worker, Licensed Marriage and Family Therapist, Psychologist, etc.)
- License number and state(s) of licensure

- Graduate education (institution, degree, year)
- Conventional certifications (e.g., EMDRIA-certified, DBT-trained, Gottman level 2, etc.)
- Evidence-informed or emerging practices being utilized (e.g., brainspotting, emotional freedom technique, somatic experience, etc.)
- Complementary and alternative trainings: Reiki level II, oracle mentorship with [teacher, date], breathwork certification, past life regression training, etc.
- If you're prelicensed, the name and credentials of your clinical supervisor

This is not just a resume flex. It's about transparency and protecting your client—and *you*. If a board ever asks how you're qualified to integrate energy psychology or intuitive tools into your clinical work, you can point to this section and say, "Right here."

The Game Changer: Where Magic Meets the Method

What truly set my informed consent apart—and gave me both clarity and confidence in my integrative approach—was the appendix I created on complementary and alternative interventions. It became the piece that made my practice feel both ethically grounded and fully aligned.

This appendix does the following:

- Clarifies how CAIs are used in conjunction with psychotherapy—not in place of it
- Names and describes each modality you integrate
- Discloses potential benefits and risks and provides clear disclaimers
- Highlights your theoretical alignment (so it's not just vibes—it's clinically grounded)

- Includes research references that back up the integration

This doesn't just cover your ass. It builds trust and models informed choice for your clients.

What This Looks Like in Practice

1) State your Integrative Clinical Practice Framework (ICPF).

- A brief client-facing description of your theoretical orientation, the beliefs that shape your work, and how change is supported in your practice (e.g., "My practice is grounded in polyvagal theory, somatic psychology, and transpersonal psychology . . ."). We built this in chapters 6, 7, and 8.

2) Name each modality used in your practice (e.g., Reiki, crystals, brainspotting). For each one, rinse and repeat the following structure:

   A) Name of modality
   B) Description paragraph (reviewed in chapter 9)
      i) What is this modality?
      ii) Where does it come from?
      iii) How is it used in your practice?
      iv) What are the potential benefits one would experience?
   C) Risks/Disclaimers (reviewed in chapter 9)
      i) What are the known risks?
      ii) Is this considered experimental or investigational by any professional body?
      iii) What should the client be aware of?

    D) Theoretical alignment (reviewed in chapter 10)
- i) Which clinical theories support your use of this practice?
- ii) How does it align with your integrative framework?

    E) Research and references (reviewed in chapter 10)
- i) At least one peer-reviewed journal article is recommended.
- ii) Also include any academic texts or books written by experts in the modality.

This appendix to your informed consent isn't just protection—it's empowerment. It allows you to use your voice, your clarity, and your training as the foundation of ethical care. It's also the perfect document to hand over to a licensing board if anyone ever challenges your work.

CAI Integration Template (Use for Each Modality)

Modality Name:

Insert the name of the complementary or alternative intervention—e.g., Reiki, tarot, sound healing, etc.

_____

Description of Each Modality and Its Clinical Application

Write a short paragraph describing what the modality is and how it is used within the context of psychotherapy. Include any sensory experiences, pacing, or ways it supports emotional or somatic processing. Highlight potential benefits.

_____

_____

_____

_____

Risks and Disclaimers

Be transparent. Outline any potential emotional, physical, or spiritual risks. Include disclaimers around boundaries, scope of the modality, optional participation, and any nonclinical aspects clients should be aware of.

_____

_____

_____

_____

Theoretical Alignment

Explain how this modality aligns with clinical theory. Name and briefly describe 2–4 clinical theories that support the integration of this practice—e.g., energy psychology, transpersonal psychology, polyvagal theory, Jungian theory, etc.

_____

_____

_____

_____

Research and References

List at least one peer-reviewed article that supports the use of this modality in mental health or related fields. You can also include reputable books, theoretical texts, or qualitative studies, but aim for at least one scholarly source.

_____

_____

_____

_____

Repeat this full structure for each modality you wish to integrate.

Emerging and Innovative Practices: The In-Between Zone

Some modalities just don't fit neatly into the usual categories. They're not officially recognized as complementary and alternative interventions (CAIs), but they're also not listed in SAMHSA's registry of empirically supported treatments. Still, these practices are widely used in clinical work, backed by years of professional experience, practitioner training, and growing (but often under-published) research.

These include modalities like emotional freedom technique (EFT), brainspotting, somatic experiencing, havening techniques, internal family systems (prior to formal recognition), polyvagal-informed interventions, sensorimotor psychotherapy, intuitive movement or embodiment work, etc.

Now, in certain states, you'll see references to these kinds of practices in the form of vague phrases scattered throughout laws, statutes, rules, or ethics codes. They might say something along these lines: "If using emerging or innovative practices, clinicians must disclose the nature of the intervention, any limitations in available research, potential risks and benefits, and ensure they are competent in its application."

That's fine. But vague compliance isn't enough. If you're going to include an emerging modality in your work—own it fully.

If you're already doing the work to write a transparent informed consent, complete the circle by giving these practices the same care and structure you would as the CAIs I just walked you through.

When you approach emerging practices with thoughtfulness, transparency, and ethical documentation, you demonstrate clinical integrity—even when the system is lagging behind you.

In a regulatory environment where the vibe is often "maybe we'll take your license, maybe we won't," it's not worth the gamble. Protect yourself. Respect your clients. And give these powerful, evolving modalities the structure they need to thrive.

Don't Forget Empirically Supported Modalities

Now let's talk about the other side of the spectrum—those therapies that are considered empirically supported or "evidence-based" (EMDR, IFS, EFT, DBT, etc.).

Just because these are recognized doesn't mean they don't need clarity in your consent—especially if you're doing something *innovative* with them.

If you're modifying an empirically supported treatment modality—say, incorporating intuitive imagery or crystal placement into your EMDR sessions—that absolutely needs to be disclosed.

Create a dedicated section titled "Empirically Supported Modalities and Enhancements" and include the following details:

- The practice (e.g., EMDR)
- A brief clinical description
- Any modifications or enhancements you bring to it
- Risks or contraindications
- Supporting research and references

Transparency ≠ liability. Transparency = integrity.

If your work is integrative, your paperwork should be integrative too.

Your informed consent isn't just about legal compliance—it's about clinical congruence. It's your opportunity to say, "This is how I practice. This is what I believe helps people heal.

And this is the care I've taken to ensure I'm doing it ethically, responsibly, and clearly."

And if that doesn't scream professional freedom, I don't know what does.

Full Circle: From Paper to Practice

Ahh. The informed consent is complete. You have a living representation of your clinical identity. A protection tool. A road map. A mirror of your integrity. But don't stop there. The goal is not to build a solid foundation only to let the rest of the house stay bare.

Your informed consent may be the legal anchor, but it's the consistency throughout your entire practice that completes the picture. The way you market your work—your website, social media, and public-facing material—should reflect the same language, ethics, and values you put in your paperwork.

Your assessment and intake process should reflect this alignment from the very beginning. Ask clients about their experiences with or interest in energy-based, spiritual, or complementary and alternative interventions (CAIs). Explore how important these practices are to their identity, culture, or healing journey, and inquire about their openness—or hesitations—toward integrative work. This not only builds trust but also sets a foundation for informed, collaborative treatment.

From there, make sure these values carry through every part of your practice. In treatment goals, explicitly name these practices as part of the therapeutic process when appropriate. In your progress or psychotherapy notes, document the use of CAIs or emerging practices as purposeful clinical interventions—not side rituals. And within your overall practice culture, create an environment where clients feel safe, seen, and informed every step of the way.

You're not just building a practice—you're creating a whole damn ecosystem. A space that holds. A space that heals. Your informed consent is the blueprint, sure—but your daily work? That's the color on the walls, the feeling in the room, the way the light pours in and says, "You're safe here."

This is how we move from fragmented to integrated.

From box checking to embodiment.

From playing defense to practicing in full transparency and power.

This is how we build trust—not just with our clients. Not just with the boards.

But with *ourselves.*

And that changes everything.

CHAPTER 12
POWER, PERMISSION, AND THE BLACK SHEEP WAY FORWARD (BAA)

Wow. Not me crying while typing this last chapter.

Why am I so emotional right now?

I had to sit with this for a minute. It's the realization that my silence is finally over. I've laid it all out in a way that makes me feel heard—like, really heard. Like I just fulfilled something deep in my bones that I didn't even know I was capable of. And now here I am.

Big-ass sigh . . . I'm seriously having a "holy shit, look at me, Mom—I freaking made it" moment.

So, from this space—not the teaching space, not the check-list space, but this raw, emotional, aligned-ass energy—I just want to talk to you. Really talk to you. Because if you've made it this far, then I already know something about you.

You're not the kind of therapist who follows rules when those rules require you to abandon yourself.

You're not here to be a cookie-cutter, manual-following version of a healer.

And let's be real—there's no way you picked up this book by accident.

Even when we know we're meant to do it differently, it's still easy to get stuck. Not because you're confused but because it's scary as hell to take up space when your truth doesn't fit the societal mold.

Here's what I want to say—clearly, directly, without the fluff . . .

Staying quiet doesn't keep you safe. It keeps you small. And that's not what you came *here* to do.

We are not here to reinforce broken systems.

We are not here to shrink, twist, or dilute what we know in our gut is real.

We are here to build. To stretch. To disrupt. To lead.

Now, it's one thing to feel that alignment in your heart. It's another thing entirely to stay grounded in that truth when someone tries to shake it.

So what happens when you start owning your approach publicly? When you post about your work online? When you say something out loud that doesn't fit neatly inside the little clinical box people expect you to stay in?

Let's start with what *doesn't* work.

Overexplaining, fearmongering, panicking that someone's going to report you, trying to out-credential the trolls, or falling into the trap of thinking you have to justify every damn decision you make.

You don't.

Here's what *does* work . . .

Respond with integrity, clarity, and a calm confidence that says, *I know what I'm doing. I know where it lives in my scope, my training, and my theory.*

And trust me—I know firsthand that holding that line isn't always easy.

As "professional" as I may be, there's still a fiery, wounded, New York Italian part of me that's always ready to pop off and set someone straight. She's got sharp words and faster reflexes—and I carry her with me everywhere. She even wrote some of these chapters.

I share this because you will get triggered. You're going to experience judgment, misunderstanding, passive-aggressive comments, and flat-out ignorance.

So when that hits? Pause.

Feel your feelings—just don't become them. Breathe. Ground. Ask yourself, Is *this my truth? What's the intention here?*

Lean in with curiosity—not to justify yourself but to assess what's real and what's projection.

Because you already know your truth. Not just the intuitive kind. The tangible kind. The kind you can name, explain, and back up with theory and training.

And from that grounded place, you get to *choose* how you respond.

You're not here to convince everyone. Some people don't want to understand what you're doing. They don't want to learn. They don't want to expand. They just want to feel right.

Let them.

You don't need to fight for a seat at a table you're actively redesigning.

Now, if you're sharing your work publicly or online, lead with education—not shame.

And remember, when you post publicly, you're not just inviting curiosity—you're also giving everyone (and their unhealed parts) a chance to respond. Saying things like "Therapists don't know what they're doing" or "This is the only trauma-informed way" might feel punchy, and it can create more resistance than resonance.

Instead, show what's possible. Show what it looks like when this work is integrated with intention. Be transparent. Be clear. Ground it in your training and your framework.

That's how we educate. That's how we shift perspectives. That's how we enhance understanding.

A question I get all the time is, "How do I handle pushback or critiques—from colleagues, boards, or keyboard warriors?"

First, let's name this: Critique isn't always a bad thing.

Some of it sharpens us. Some of it pushes us to clarify, to refine, to grow.

But not all of it deserves your energy.

So, when someone questions your approach, ask yourself,

Are they genuinely curious?
Are they projecting their own fear or rigidity?
Are they using shame to try to control the conversation?

You are never required to prove yourself to someone who leads with judgment instead of inquiry. Instead, respond with discernment and boundaries.

Here's a simple script you can hold in your back pocket . . .

"That's a great question. I'm happy to share how my work aligns with my ethics, scope of practice, and clinical theory—but only if we're having a respectful conversation."

Or . . .

"I've done the work to ensure what I do is both ethical and effective. If you're curious about the research or frameworks behind it, I'm happy to point you in that direction."

And my personal favorite, when someone tries to call something "unethical" without receipts:

"Can you point me to where that's written in statute, code, or admin law? I take ethics seriously—and I don't rely on hearsay or opinion to guide my practice."

You don't owe anyone a performance to prove you're ethical.

You don't need to explain every move to make it valid.

You are not unethical because you're innovative.

You are not unsafe because you're expansive.

You are not wrong for doing it differently.

You *are* part of the larger collective that came to shift the consciousness of this world.

You've Done the Work. Now Be the Work.

Okay, now back to the teaching space.

You've read the framework.

You've mapped your theory.

You've clarified your language.

You've built consent, not just to protect your license but to claim your power.

I would like to remind you of what I hope you already know.

You don't need to ask for permission. You already have it.

You're allowed to practice with intuition.

You're allowed to lead with energy.

You're allowed to reference ancestors, spirit, ritual, and root work—and still be ethical.

You're allowed to build a practice that looks nothing like the textbook—and everything like your truth.

But here's the key: You're *not* allowed to do it sloppily.

This book has given you the tools to do it ethically, legally, and with clinical grounding. So now go use them.

Let go . . .

Of the lie that being different makes you dangerous.

Of the fear that playing by their rules is the only way to stay safe.

Of the shame that says your practice must look like someone else's to be valid.

You are already valid.

You are already whole.

You are already ready.

This is your permission slip. In fact, go ahead and sign on the line below—your way of giving yourself the green light to live and serve others with authenticity and confidence:

X _____

Now, don't confuse permission with passivity.

We are not here to quietly "fit in." We are here to reshape the room.

The truth is that the field is shifting whether we lead it or not. So the question becomes, Will we sit back and let outdated frameworks decide what "helping" looks like? Or will we lead with depth, nuance, and backbone—and create a new way forward?

One of my favorite things about working with other Black Sheep therapists?

That *untapped* energy. That raw, holy-shit-it's-happening boldness that lives just beneath the fear, and there is a reason that fear runs so deep.

So many of us inherited a professional legacy built on silence.

On obedience.

On *don't make waves.*

We were trained to comply, not to challenge. Told we had to prove ourselves over and over again just to be trusted. And we internalized the idea that if we got too bold, too creative, too spiritual, too *real*—we'd lose everything.

But that fear is not yours!

It's generational.

It's systemic.

And it's no longer serving you.

So let's talk about how to move this revolution forward—in real, tangible ways.

1. Engage in Research (Yes, You Can)

Start evaluating your own work, write up your own case studies, track patterns, document outcomes. Research doesn't have to be a university-only thing. You don't need an institutional review board (IRB) to reflect on your method, your data, your results. There are programs, mentors, and support communities to help you design your own qualitative or theoretical research—without needing another degree to "legitimize" what you already know.

You're already sitting on gold—give yourself permission to mine it.

Need inspiration? Look at Candice Rasa, LCSW, an incredible therapist who (at the time of this book) is conducting a mixed-methods research study on the Akashic Records and their impact on mental health outcomes. A literal badass.

This is how we start building empirical support for spiritual and energy-based practices: We study what we love and what we're already doing.

2. Name the Framework No One Else Has

Just because no one has named it yet doesn't mean it isn't real.

You can be the one to build the framework.

To give language to what others have felt but never mapped. To carve out new terrain for others to walk on.

Don't believe me? Look at Dr. Margaret Arnd-Caddigan, PhD, LCSW, and her brilliant mind-centered depth approach for healing—a clinical model that integrates intuition and soul-level work with practical tools and methods. Her approach offers structured, research-informed ways to ethically bring spirituality into therapy. She didn't wait for someone else to create a framework that honored her way of knowing.

She *became* the framework.

You have the same permission.

Take it.

3. Teach What You Know

If you know your theory, understand your scope, can articulate your integration clearly—why not teach it?

- Create a CEU course.
- Host a workshop.
- Run a webinar.
- Offer consultation.
- Build a coaching program that bridges the clinical and the spiritual.

In other words, fill the gap! So many spiritual and energy-based modality trainings are being taught by brilliant spiritual practitioners—but not therapists. Which is why clinicians often leave these trainings inspired but confused, wondering, *How the hell do I bring this into my actual practice?*

That's where you come in.

In fact, it's exactly why I created the Black Sheep Therapist® Academy—a CEU platform *only* focused on trainings you'd never find on traditional sites.

We've got courses on Reiki, complementary and alternative interventions, integrative documentation, ethics in unconventional practice, and more.

This work deserves a seat at the continuing education table, and therapists deserve support in integrating it responsibly.

You don't have to wait for an invitation.

You can build the table.

4. Expand Your Reach

Submit to conferences.

Write articles.

Pitch keynotes.

Speak your truth louder and in more rooms.

You don't have to be everywhere.

But it's time to stop hiding.

Let the world see what integrative, rooted, ethical, soul-aligned therapy actually looks like.

And if you're scared you won't get picked? Welcome to the club—I'm the president.

I've lost count of how many times I've been rejected by conferences, summits, podcasts, or panels. At this point, I treat them like little trophies—receipts that remind me exactly who's not ready for this kind of work.

And honestly? That's information. It keeps me from wasting energy trying to squeeze into rooms that were never built to hold this level of depth.

But make no mistake—I'll never stop showing up.

Because I'm not here to fit in. I'm here to shift the damn system.

5. Refine Your Niche

You don't have to water down your work to attract clients; in fact, the clearer you are, the easier it is for the right clients to find you.

I want you to choose clients who align with your beliefs about change and transformation, who honor your ethics, who match your energy, who are ready for the kind of work you were born to do.

Own your space.

Stop apologizing for it.

Let your people choose you.

You are the future of mental health care.

And the work you do—when it's done in alignment, with grounding and integrity—is a literal blueprint for the evolution of this field.

The mic is already in your hand—speak!

And I will help you build it.

The Innovative Practitioner Accelerator Program

I hope you're just as fired up at the end of this book as you were when you first opened it. I hope this book has landed for you in a way that makes you feel seen, heard, and deeply inspired.

Because that was the whole point.

I've given you the full picture—outlines, language, and strategies for how to move forward with clinical integrity and ethical alignment, even when you're integrating practices that the field still side-eyes.

We've walked through how to meet the vague-ass standards of statutes, admin codes, ethics regulations, and professional expectations—and do it all without watering yourself down.

But sometimes a framework isn't enough.

Sometimes you need a *container*—a space to walk this out, step by step, with real support, feedback, and expert eyes on your practice.

That's why I created the Innovative Practitioner Accelerator (IPA) Program.

This program is the living, breathing version of everything I mapped out in this book—but on steroids.

It's where your ideas stop living on paper and start showing up in your policies, your language, your confidence, and your bank account. It's where we take all of the *how* and *why* you've just learned and turn it into *now* and *done*—in your practice, your systems, and your mindset.

Inside the Innovative Practitioner Accelerator Program, we don't just talk about integration—we build it. You'll create your own customized informed consent, align your modalities with clinical theory, clean up your documentation, and learn how to talk about your work with the same authority you already feel in your soul. It's not a course you watch; it's an evolution you experience. Because when you leave, you won't just understand ethical integration—you'll *embody* it.

And if I were to list *everything* inside the IPA, I'd basically be writing a second book.

So instead, let me give you the *essence* of the program that is changing the lives of spiritual practitioners everywhere. If you decide to join them, here's what you'll experience:

1. Deep Personal Reflection + Theoretical Alignment

We always start where it matters most—*you*. Your story. Your values. Your lived experience. Then we reverse-engineer your unique clinical identity and walk you through the full development of your Integrative Clinical Practice Framework (ICPF)—complete with clearly aligned clinical theories that reflect *how* you work with clients. If you need to refresh your memory, head back to chapter 8.

2. Niche Clarity + Empowered Marketing

We're not doing cookie-cutter bios here. We craft language that is client-centered, ethics-compliant, and soul-aligned. Your niche isn't just about your population—it's about your *why*, your theory, and the kind of transformation you facilitate. You'll finally be able to explain your work in a way that feels good *and* makes sense to boards, clients, and referral partners—and, most importantly, call in your ideal clients!

3. Professional + State-Specific Informed Consent

This isn't just a template. And it's definitely not just a download-and-go.

In this step, we roll up our sleeves and review your specific state statutes, licensing board rules, and ethics codes—together. Then we build your informed consent from the ground up, making sure it's not only regulatory sound but spiritually honest and clinically aligned.

You'll learn how to name your approach, your methods, and your scope of practice in clear, empowered language—without diluting your work or shrinking yourself to fit outdated expectations.

This is where we blend the clinical with the spiritual, fusing both in your Complementary and Alternative Interventions Appendix. Need a refresher on how we build this fusion? Head back to chapters 9–11, where I walked you through the Clinical Fusion Blueprint.

And don't worry—you're not doing this alone. I'm right beside you the whole way.

Because this isn't just about ticking regulatory boxes.

It's about protecting your work, claiming your truth, and making sure your documentation reflects the actual magic you bring into the room—without compromising your ethics or your soul.

4. Clinical Documentation That Reflects Your Approach

From assessment to intake to treatment planning, we help you build documentation that mirrors your method.

We make sure your paperwork includes prompts that match your clinical theory and give you language to justify practices like energy work, intuitive guidance, ancestral healing, or nature-based interventions—all in alignment with clinical outcomes.

5. Practice Protection: Regulatory + Ethical Templates

Touch disclaimers? Covered.

Consent for intensives? Got it.

Website terms, privacy policy, group therapy agreements, supervision contracts? Yep.

You'll get access to a full library of customizable templates designed to protect your practice and reflect your scope.

And honestly, if you ask anyone who has taken my IPA program—if I don't have it, I will help you build it.

6. Live Support, Empowerment Coaching, and Community

This isn't some faceless course you complete in isolation. You get an entire ecosystem of support:

- *1:1 coaching* to get direct feedback and strategic clarity
- *Live group calls* to workshop your language, framework, and systems

- *Empowerment coaches* (real IPA grads!) and industry experts to walk with you every step of the way
- *Money mindset trainings* to unpack your relationship with worth, value, and pricing
- Access to CE courses through the *Black Sheep Therapist Academy*, including topics like Reiki in Clinical Practice, Integrative Documentation, Complementary and Alternative Interventions, and more.
- A dedicated, like-minded community of fellow clinicians who've invested in this work—because building a bold, integrative practice is easier (and way more powerful) when you don't do it alone.

And yes—there's a robust digital course library you can move through at your own pace.

But it's the community that makes this powerful. The relationships that form. The collaborations that continue. The way therapists light up when they finally feel like they don't have to translate their soul into someone else's language.

Finally, because one-size-fits-all doesn't work for Black Sheep therapists, your path should fit *you*, which is why you can also take advantage of any of the following:

- A *Done-for-You Informed Consent service* to take the guesswork (and the legal panic) out of paperwork
- An *Identify Your Theory Masterclass* to help you get grounded in your unique clinical alignment right from the start
- And more tools, trainings, and offerings on the way—because this movement is just getting started.

And just so you know . . . I'm *always* building. Always expanding. Always thinking about what you'll need next.

So what I've shared with you in this book? It's just the beginning. A drop in the bucket.

By the time you're ready to take a chance on yourself, there might be even more waiting for you. So don't hold me to this exact list—but do trust this: If I haven't built the thing you need yet, I'm probably building it now.

Book a free strategy call with me or my team to explore all our options and see if the IPA is the right fit for you by visiting www.theblacksheepguide.com.

We're ready when you are.

Real Words. Real Wins. From Real Black Sheep Therapists

If you're reading this and a voice inside is whispering,

Yeah . . . this all sounds amazing, but—

I see you.

That *but* can be loud.

It sounds like . . .

Do I really have the time?

Do I really have the money?

Am I even worth investing in?

I've been there too.

That hesitation is human. It's the echo of every system that told us to play small, to wait until we were "ready."

But here's what I learned:

The only thing I can't afford anymore is not investing in myself.

There will *always* be another reason to wait.

Another excuse to stay safe, quiet, uncertain.

But ask yourself, Where has that pattern gotten you?

Every Black Sheep therapist I've worked with started in that same *but*.

Then they said *yes*.

And what came next wasn't just confidence—it was *freedom*.

Here's what that freedom looks like in real life.

"I'm not hiding anymore."

Michelle Scott, MS, LPC, RMT

www.healingwithmeesh.com

I finally stopped gaslighting myself about being *that* therapist—the one who mixes Reiki, oracle cards, HSP work, and Human Design right into session. I used to spiral over whether this was "allowed" or if some licensing boogeyman was going to bust down my door. Now? Different story. With airtight informed consent, treatment plans that actually align theory with practice, and proof from other badass therapists doing the same—it's game over for that fear. My anxiety is gone. My notes are clear. My practice has a waitlist. Clients come to me because they want therapy with the spiritual sauce.

Honestly? It's like I deleted a giant malware file of fear and doubt from my brain. Now I can finally run at full speed. I feel untouchable—ethically, creatively, and personally. I'm aligned, I'm lit up, and I'm not hiding anymore.

"Now I have the wisdom to live the life I always wanted to co-create with the Universe."

Vanessa-Gissele Holliman, LCSW
www.beingwhol-istic.com

Never in a million years did I think a group coaching program could transform both my personal and professional life this deeply. I joined IPA thinking I'd learn how to articulate my integrative modalities—astrology, ritual, oracle cards, sound therapy, holistic nutrition—but what I actually found was my full potential. The question is no longer "'Can I?" It's "How will I?" I now have the language, confidence, and clarity to ethically integrate every tool that makes my work powerful. I transitioned my practice into a nonprofit, started creating CEUs to empower other clinicians, and have my first waitlist ever.

I've always had the drive; now I have the wisdom to cocreate the life I've always envisioned—with the Universe as my business partner.

"The progress I have witnessed in my clients has been remarkable."

Samantha Schalk, LMSW
www.guardianclinicalessentials.com

Before completing the IPA, I stayed inside the lines. I only used what felt "safe"—mindfulness, guided meditation, EFT, somatic work—because I was afraid to go further. I didn't believe I could ethically integrate other energy-based interventions into traditional therapy frameworks.

Now I can confidently explain, to clients, colleagues, and even insurance providers, exactly how these practices fit within clinical theory. My sessions now weave together Emotion Code, Body Code, Belief Code, the Akashic Records, Reiki, ancestral healing, and brainspotting in ways that honor both ethics and intuition.

The progress I've witnessed in my clients has been remarkable. I show up more authentically, my practice has grown beyond what I thought possible, and my confidence is unshakable. This work no longer feels like a risk—it feels like my purpose.

This experience also reignited a passion for entrepreneurship, and the program encouraged me to dive deeper into the business side of private practice. That inspiration, combined with my supervisory background and strong protective instincts, led me to start a new business called Guardian Clinical Essentials, LLC. It is dedicated to helping mental health professionals strengthen their compliance, systems, and practice protection.

"My business is filled with clients that are the ideal fit for me—and me for them."

Tasha Lawson, LPC, CHT
www.tashamarielawson.com

Before IPA, I had a deep longing to bring the modalities I loved into therapy but didn't know if it was possible—or how to frame it in a way that honored regulations. Now I do.

I feel confident and excited about the integrative work

I offer, and my clients want exactly that kind of support. My caseload is full of ideal-fit clients who match my energy and approach. I'm energized again about therapy, deeply fulfilled by my work, and inspired by what my clients and I create together.

For the first time in years, I feel like my business and my soul are on the same page.

"I feel more grounded, more authentic, and more empowered."

Johanna Padilla, LMFT
www.clinicallyjohanna.com

One thing I now feel confident doing, thanks to IPA, is integrating my psychic, mediumship, and energy work with therapy—ethically and transparently. I used to second-guess whether I could bring these worlds together, but now my paperwork, consent forms, and practice policies reflect exactly how I work.

That alignment has changed everything. My clients feel safer, I feel more grounded, and my confidence as both a therapist and intuitive practitioner has expanded. I finally stopped fragmenting myself and started practicing as the whole, authentic me.

I'm no longer walking a tightrope—I'm walking my path.

"I can speak confidently about what I do as a healer and therapist."

Amber Tolbert, LCSW
www.healersinpractice.com

My group practice uses a comprehensive model for treating generational trauma, where trauma recovery naturally overlaps with spiritual identity and awareness. Through IPA, I learned how to integrate clear, ethical language in my marketing and consents to reflect the modalities and theories that support whole-person healing—physical, mental, emotional, and spiritual.

Inner child healing is a sacred practice that extends beyond theory, and IPA helped me speak about it with confidence, integrity, and alignment. I now feel grounded in naming my work as both a therapist and a healer, and I can share my own experiences in a way that supports, not overshadows, my clients.

I hold space. I shine the flashlight. And I do it with both compassion and clarity.

"I show up more authentically, aligned, and unafraid."

Christina Baisden, LMSW/LCSW
www.willowsagecounseling.com

Before IPA, I never imagined I could share my personal story—my trauma, my struggles, my connection with nature and spirituality—with my clients or colleagues. I thought professionalism meant separation.

Now I see authenticity as the most ethical choice I can make. My clients, my family, my colleagues—and most importantly, I—all engage with the truest version of me. That alignment has made me a better clinician and a more fulfilled human.

Because I live and speak my truth, my light shines brighter. I no longer fear being seen.

Now It's Your Turn

Every therapist you just read about began with a question: *Can I really do this my way?*

And every single one of them found the same answer: Yes!

Not because they broke the rules but because they finally understood the rules well enough to move within them—freely.

This isn't just professional success.

It's what happens when integrity and intuition stop competing.

When one therapist steps into alignment, the system itself starts to shift.

But let's be clear—as much as this movement is about freedom, it's also about responsibility. Part of our ethical obligation as therapists isn't just to follow existing models but to help *shift* them when they no longer serve the field.

Systems don't wake up one day and say, "You know what? I think I could be doing better."

They change because the people within them apply pressure—not through shame, not through screaming into the void, but through understanding, reflection, and courageous innovation.

Because just like your own healing, you can't transform something you refuse to understand.

I don't believe the mental health system is total bullshit.

We *need* regulations.

We *need* accountability.

We *need* ethical safeguards to protect clients from exploitation, harm, or misuse of power.

But we also need therapists who are willing to look at the system with clear eyes and say, "This part works. That part doesn't. Let's evolve it."

That's what ethical practice really is—not blind obedience, not reckless rebellion, but conscious participation in something bigger than yourself.

When we engage the field with reflection, awareness, and courage—when we challenge, reimagine, and create new applications—we don't just protect our licenses.

We advance the profession.

That's the legacy of the Black Sheep therapist: not rebellion for the sake of it, but revolution through remembrance—of who you *are*, what you *know*, and why you came *here*.

ACKNOWLEDGMENTS

To every therapist who's ever been told they were too much, too spiritual, too intuitive, or not clinical enough—you weren't the problem. You were the preview.

To the students of the Innovative Practitioner Accelerator Program and The Black Sheep Therapist Community—thank you for keeping the fire of this work alive. You are living proof that integrity and innovation not only can coexist but thrive together. You are the future of mental health.

To my husband, John, who has loved me through every evolution, and to our son, Anthony Raffaele, the sweetest part of my life—you're both the best parts of my story.

References

Alabama Legislature. 2024. *Code of Alabama*. Title 34, Chapter 30: Social Work Practice. Montgomery: Alabama Legislature. https://www.legislature.state.al.us.

American Association for Marriage and Family Therapy. 2015. AAMFT *Code of Ethics*. Alexandria, VA: AAMFT. https://www.aamft.org/Legal_Ethics/Code_of_Ethics.aspx.

American Counseling Association. 2014. ACA *Code of Ethics*. Alexandria, VA: ACA. https://www.counseling.org/resources/aca-code-of-ethics.pdf.

American Psychological Association. 2017. *Ethical Principles of Psychologists and Code of Conduct*. Washington, DC: APA. https://www.apa.org/ethics/code.

American Psychological Association Presidential Task Force on Evidence-Based Practice. 2006. "Evidence-Based Practice in Psychology." *American Psychologist* 61 (4): 271–285. https://doi.org/10.1037/0003-066X.61.4.271.

Ansbacher, Heinz L., and Rowena R. Ansbacher, eds. 1964. *The Individual Psychology of Alfred Adler*. New York: HarperCollins.

Armson, Alison, Cathy Hodgetts, Amanda Wright, Amy Jacques, Teresa Ricciardi, Giulia Bettinelli, and Benjamin Walker. 2019. "Knowledge, Beliefs, and Influences Associated with Complementary and Alternative Medicine among Physiotherapy and

Counselling Students." *Physiotherapy Research International* 24 (4): e1825. https://doi.org/10.1002/pri.1825.

Astin, John A. 1998. "Why Patients Use Alternative Medicine: Results of a National Study." JAMA 279 (19): 1548–1553. https://doi.org/10.1001/jama.279.19.1548.

Aveni, Elena, Beat Bauer, Anne-Sylvie Ramelet, Isabelle Decosterd, Pierre Ballabeni, Esther Bonvin, and Pierre-Yves Rodondi. 2017. "Healthcare Professionals' Sources of Knowledge of Complementary Medicine in an Academic Center." PLOS ONE 12 (9): e0184979. https://doi.org/10.1371/journal.pone.0184979.

Bishop, Felicity L., and George T. Lewith. 2010. "Who Uses CAM? A Narrative Review of Demographic Characteristics and Health Factors Associated with CAM Use." *Evidence-Based Complementary and Alternative Medicine* 7 (1): 11–28. https://doi.org/10.1093/ecam/nen023.

Butt, Trevor, and Bill Warren. 2015. "Personal Construct Theory and Philosophy." In *The Wiley Handbook of Personal Construct Psychology*, edited by David A. Winter and Nick Reed, 11–22. Chichester, UK: Wiley-Blackwell. https://doi.org/10.1002/9781118508728.ch2.

California Board of Behavioral Sciences. 2023. "Laws and Regulations." Accessed October 12, 2025. https://www.bbs.ca.gov.

California Board of Behavioral Sciences. n.d. *Dual Relationships*. Sacramento, CA: California Department of Consumer Affairs. Accessed October 12, 2025. https://www.bbs.ca.gov.

Castelnuovo, Gianluca. 2004. "A Critical Review of Empirically Supported Treatments (ESTs) and Common Factors Perspective in Psychotherapy." *ResearchGate*. https://www.researchgate.net/publication/242218788.

Cherniack, Edward P., Rachel S. Senzel, and Chunxiao Pan. 2008. "Correlates of Use of Alternative Medicine by the Elderly in an Urban Population." *Journal of Alternative and Complementary Medicine* 7 (3): 277–280. https://doi.org/10.1089/10755530360623379.

Clarke, Tainya C., Lindsey I. Black, Barbara J. Stussman, Patricia M. Barnes, and Richard L. Nahin. 2015. *Trends in the Use of Com-*

plementary Health Approaches among Adults: United States, 2002–2012. *National Health Statistics Reports*, no. 79. Hyattsville, MD: National Center for Health Statistics. https://www.cdc.gov/nchs/data/nhsr/nhsr079.pdf.

Clossey, Laurene, Mark D. DiLauro, Jessica P. Edwards, Chia Hu, Hilary Pazaki, Aimee Monge, and Kathryn Smart. 2023. "Complementary and Alternative Medicine (CAM) Use among Mental Health Consumers." *Community Mental Health Journal* 59 (6): 1549–1559. https://doi.org/10.1007/s10597-023-01142-w.

Corey, Gerald. 2017. *Theory and Practice of Counseling and Psychotherapy.* 10th ed. Boston: Cengage Learning.

DeSylvia, Dana, Mady Stuber, Carol C. Fung, Shahrzad Bazargan-Hejazi, and Edwin Cooper. 2011. "The Knowledge, Attitudes and Usage of Complementary and Alternative Medicine of Medical Students." *Evidence-Based Complementary and Alternative Medicine* 2011: 728902. https://doi.org/10.1093/ecam/nen075.

Deal, Kathleen Holtz. 2007. "Psychodynamic Theory." *Advances in Social Work* 8 (1). https://doi.org/10.18060/140.

El-Olemy, A. T., N. M. Radwan, N. S. E. Shihab, and W. M. Dawood. 2014. "Knowledge, Attitudes, and Practices of Non-Medical Students in Traditional and Complementary Medicine in Gharbiya Governorate, Egypt: A Cross-Sectional Study." *Forschende Komplementärmedizin/Research in Complementary Medicine* 21 (5): 314–319. https://doi.org/10.1159/000367979.

Feinstein, David, and Donna Eden. 2008. *Energy Psychology: Self-Healing Practices for Bodymind Health.* New York: Tarcher/Penguin.

Flexner, Abraham. 1910. *Medical Education in the United States and Canada: A Report to the Carnegie Foundation for the Advancement of Teaching.* Bulletin No. 4. New York: Carnegie Foundation.

Florida Board of Clinical Social Work, Marriage and Family Therapy, and Mental Health Counseling. 2023. "Statutes and Rules." Accessed October 12, 2025. https://floridasmentalhealthprofessions.gov.

Florida Legislature. 2024. *Florida Statutes*. Title XXXII, Chapter 491: Clinical, Counseling, and Psychotherapy Services. Tallahassee: Florida Legislature.

Gitz-Johansen, Thomas. 2016. "Jung in Education: A Review of Historical and Contemporary Contributions from Analytical Psychology to the Field of Education." *Journal of Analytical Psychology* 61 (3): 365–384.

Hanney, Stephen R., Miguel A. Gonzalez-Block, Muir Gray, Martin Kogan, and Jonathan Buxton. 2015. "The Utilization of Health Research in Policy-Making: Concepts, Examples and Methods of Assessment." *Health Research Policy and Systems* 13 (1): 27. https://doi.org/10.1186/s12961-015-0004-7.

Hartley, Linda. 2004. *Somatic Psychology: Body, Mind and Meaning*. Chichester, UK: John Wiley & Sons.

Hayes, Steven C., Dermot Barnes-Holmes, and Bryan Roche, eds. 2001. *Relational Frame Theory: A Post-Skinnerian Account of Human Language and Cognition*. New York: Kluwer Academic/Plenum Publishers.

Hayes, Steven C., Kirk D. Strosahl, and Kelly G. Wilson. 1999. *Acceptance and Commitment Therapy: An Experiential Approach to Behavior Change*. New York: Guilford Press.

Institute of Medicine (U.S.), ed. 2005. *Complementary and Alternative Medicine in the United States*. Washington, DC: National Academies Press.

Islahudin, Farida, Izyan A. Shahdan, and Siti M. Mohamad-Samuri. 2017. "Association between Belief and Attitude toward Preference of Complementary Alternative Medicine Use." *Patient Preference and Adherence* 11: 913–918. https://doi.org/10.2147/PPA.S132282.

Johnson, Paula J., Judy Jou, Deborah M. Upchurch, and Fan Wu Cheng. 2018. "Perceived Benefits of Using Complementary and Alternative Medicine by Race/Ethnicity among Midlife and Older Adults in the United States." *Journal of Aging and Health* 30 (1): 113–133. https://doi.org/10.1177/0898264316678676.

Linehan, Marsha M. 1993. *Cognitive-Behavioral Treatment of Borderline Personality Disorder.* New York: Guilford Press.

Linehan, Marsha M. 2015. *DBT® Skills Training Manual.* 2nd ed. New York: Guilford Press.

Lilienfeld, Scott O. 2013. "Why Many Clinical Psychologists Are Resistant to Evidence-Based Practice." *Clinical Psychology Review* 33 (7): 883–900. https://doi.org/10.1016/j.cpr.2013.05.004.

Maryland Board of Professional Counselors and Therapists. 2023. "COMAR 10.58.03.10 – Physical Contact." Accessed October 12, 2025. https://health.maryland.gov/bopc.

McEwen, Shelly. 2015. "Social Work in Health Care When Conventional Meets Complementary: Nonspecific Back Pain and Massage Therapy." *Health & Social Work* 40 (1): 19–25. https://doi.org/10.1093/hsw/hlu041.

McFadden, Kathleen L., Tiffany D. Hernández, and Tiffany A. Ito. 2010. "Attitudes Toward Complementary and Alternative Medicine Influence Its Use." *Explore* (NY) 6 (6): 380–388. https://doi.org/10.1016/j.explore.2010.08.004.

Minnesota Legislature. 2024. *Minnesota Statutes.* Chapter 148B: Mental Health Services. St. Paul: Minnesota Legislature.

National Association of Social Workers. 2021. *Code of Ethics of the National Association of Social Workers.* Washington, DC: NASW Press. https://www.socialworkers.org/About/Ethics/Code-of-Ethics.

National Center for Complementary and Integrative Health (NCCIH). "Complementary, Alternative, or Integrative Health: What's in a Name?" Accessed September 25, 2020. https://www.nccih.nih.gov/health/complementary-alternative-or-integrative-health-whats-in-a-name.

New York State Education Department. n.d. *Rules of the Board of Regents: §52.32–33 Licensed Mental Health Practitioners.* Albany, NY: Author. Accessed October 12, 2025. https://www.op.nysed.gov.

New York State Office of the Professions. n.d. "Maintaining Appropriate Professional Boundaries." Accessed October 12, 2025. https://www.op.nysed.gov.

Porges, Stephen W. 2022. "Polyvagal Theory: A Science of Safety." *Frontiers in Integrative Neuroscience* 16: 871227. https://doi.org/10.3389/fnint.2022.871227.

Sakaluk, John K., Alexander F. Williams, Kaitlyn M. Kilshaw, and Scott O. Lilienfeld. 2019. "Evaluating the Evidential Value of Empirically Supported Psychotherapies." *Journal of Abnormal Psychology* 128 (6): 534–547. https://doi.org/10.1037/abn0000421.

Schneider, Reyna A. 2020. "Beyond the Lab: Empirically Supported Treatments in Community Settings." *Frontiers in Psychology* 11 (1969). https://doi.org/10.3389/fpsyg.2020.01969.

Shapiro, Francine. 2001. *Eye Movement Desensitization and Reprocessing: Basic Principles, Protocols, and Procedures*. 2nd ed. New York: Guilford Press.

Shapiro, Francine. 2017. *Eye Movement Desensitization and Reprocessing (EMDR) Therapy: Basic Principles, Protocols, and Procedures*. 3rd ed. New York: Guilford Press.

Sue, Stanley, Nolan W. Zane, Gordon C. Hall, and Frederick T. Berger. 2009. "The Case for Cultural Competency in Psychotherapeutic Interventions." *Annual Review of Psychology* 60 (1): 525–548. https://doi.org/10.1146/annurev.psych.60.110707.163651.

Texas Behavioral Health Executive Council. 2023. "Rules and Regulations." Accessed October 12, 2025. https://www.bhec.texas.gov.

Vitolo, Tina, Morgan E. Cooley, and Darren Weissman. 2023. "Licensed Clinical Social Workers' Perceptions of Complementary and Alternative Interventions." *Research on Social Work Practice*. https://doi.org/10.1177/10497315231195829.

Wertz, Frederick J. 2023. "The History of Humanistic and Existential Psychology: The Possibility and Cultural Contexts of Renewal in Science." In APA *Handbook of Humanistic and Existential Psychology*, edited by Louis Hoffman, David A. Leech, Dan Hocoy, and Edward DeRobertis, 17–39. London: APA Books.

Zapata, K. 2020. "Decolonizing Mental Health: The Importance of an Oppression-Focused Mental Health System." *Calgary Journal*. February 27, 2020. https://www.calgaryjournal.ca.

ABOUT THE AUTHOR

Dr. Tina Vitolo, LCSW, DSW, is a licensed clinical social worker, rebel educator, and founder of The Black Sheep Therapist—a movement and mentorship platform for clinicians who refuse to shrink their practice to fit outdated boxes. With nearly 20 years of experience, Tina helps therapists ethically integrate spiritual, energy-based, and nontraditional modalities into clinical care without compromising integrity or licensure.

She earned her doctorate in social work from Florida Atlantic University in 2022, where her article entitled "Perceptions of Complementary and Alternative Interventions among LCSWs" was published in the *Journal of Research on Social Work Practice*. Frustrated by the lack of clear guidance, Tina created what the field was missing—a concrete framework for ethical, clinically grounded integration for spiritual and energy-based modalities. She's the creator of the Innovative Practitioner Accelerator, a first-of-its-kind program that teaches therapists how to align their personal healing tools with clinical theory, legal documentation, and ethical standards.

Tina also leads The Black Sheep Therapist Facebook group, a community of thousands of therapists who are reclaiming their voice, purpose, and professional freedom.

Her mission? To help therapists stop hiding their magic and start building practices that reflect the full truth of who they are—with confidence, clarity, and compliance.

To connect with Tina, visit her online:

www.theblacksheepguide.com
Instagram: @the_blacksheep_therapist
TikTok: @theblacksheeptherapist

www.ingramcontent.com/pod-product-compliance
Lightning Source LLC
Chambersburg PA
CBHW022053020426
42335CB00012B/669